.

MAKE A PAYMENT

HOW TO DECIMATE CREDIT CARDS WITH DEBT CONSOLIDATION TO OBTAIN FINANCIAL PEACE OF MIND

J.C. ALLEN

CONTENTS

HOW TO GET THE MOST OUT OF
THIS BOOK

If you're genuinely curious, willing to make changes, and take action, you can be on your way towards a debt-free future. To help you on your journey, I have created a free workbook that includes an easy to use budgeting sheet & debt calculator to determine your debt-free date. Use this tool to guide you in accomplishing your goals.

To get the most out of this book, sign up now by visiting the link below:

https://allenanything.com

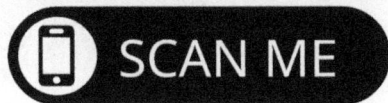

INTRODUCTION

"You must gain control over your money or the lack of it will forever control you."

— DAVE RAMSEY

If you're anything like the millions of people who are stressed out about their finances, you know what it's like to feel like you're trapped under a mountain of debt with no way out. This is something I've experienced as well, both in my own life and growing up watching my mother struggle financially. We weren't a wealthy family and debt only made this worse. My mother worked three minimum wage jobs just to put food on the table and even as a kid, I could see how much stress could come from being unable to escape financial troubles.

Debt, whether it comes from student loans, auto loans, mortgages, or credit cards, takes its toll on your physical and mental health. Financial stress can lead you to lay awake at night worrying about whether or not you'll be able to afford next month's rent, and never having enough money means you might make less healthy nutritional choices simply because they're cheaper. Debt can also interfere with your ability to live your life how you want. For example, a poor credit score caused by credit card debt can make it harder to get approved for future lines of credit. You might not qualify for a home loan, or you might end up with a subprime loan rate for your next car, meaning the interest rate is higher than average. High interest rates mean you're even more likely to get stuck in the cycle of debt. In short, debt can quickly spiral out of your control if you let it.

Despite how powerless you might feel, you always have the ability to dig yourself out of debt, no matter how much you owe. Debt consolidation is a powerful tool for regaining control over your finances. When it's used alongside strategies like repayment plans and better borrowing habits, you can start paying off your credit card debt and anything else you owe, letting you achieve true financial peace of mind. In *Make a Payment*, you'll learn how to use these methods and many more to eliminate debt, improve your credit score, and enjoy a more stress-free life.

By revamping how you use credit, you can free yourself from debt and also prevent yourself from getting back into the same bad habits that led to money troubles in the first place. Credit cards are a slippery slope because they enable you to buy more than you can afford. If you can't make payments, your interest builds, and suddenly that purchase that was only a little out of your price range is now the catalyst for wrecking your credit. However, if you start using credit cards as a tool rather than relying on them as a crutch, you can build your credit instead of decimating it. This allows you to escape your debt problems while also keeping future financial issues at bay. You'll learn the best methods for making credit work for you, not the other way around. As a result, you'll never have to spend another day stressed about your finances.

I want to help you escape debt because I went through the same difficulties managing my finances when no one else had taught me about money management. After growing up in a household where my mother constantly worked just to pay off never-ending bills, I knew I had to break this cycle for myself and my family. I studied mathematics in college and went on to pursue a career in finance. Before graduating, I got into plenty of debt troubles of my own, with both student loans and credit cards. I worked four part-time jobs while I attended school, including tutoring in the math department, which gave me insight into how misunderstanding issues can take a toll on your life and how people learn about money matters and more. My goal in writing this book isn't strictly to teach you how to manage your money; it's also to show you how to acquaint yourself and internalize these lessons as you get yourself out of debt.

Since my university days, I have spent over a decade in the financial services industry, working at just about every position available at multiple financial institutions. These include loan processing, treasury and cash management, and accounting. I've spent time at credit unions, banks, and major online lenders, getting a feel for all parts of the industry and how different credit lenders operate. I've seen both the front and back ends of the loan consolidation process. I know the ins and outs of the financial industry and I know them from personal experience. This is why I am so confident that everyone can get started down the path to financial freedom with the correct information and the right action plan.

This book includes many of the same lessons I learned that helped me and many others escape debt. Even though I experienced massive debt, I was able to find a way out, which has only made me more passionate about helping others consolidate their credit card debt and successfully pay off what they owe. With this information, you too can make credit card debt a thing of the past.

You've spent enough of your life worrying about money troubles. It's time to start making payments so you can take back control of your wallet and your life.

1

WHAT MAKES DEBT DEVASTATING?

"The one thing that offends me the most is when I walk by a bank and see ads trying to convince people to take out second mortgages on their home so they can go on vacation. That's approaching evil."

— JEFF BEZOS

Debt is at its most dangerous when you don't know enough about it to use it safely and effectively. The less you know about sound credit card and loan repayment practices, the greater your risk of falling into bad spending habits, which can turn small expenses into huge problems. To overcome your difficulties with debt, you must understand what it is and the many ways it can negatively impact your life.

WHAT IS DEBT?

In broad terms, debt is an amount of money borrowed by one party from another that needs to be repaid and typically used as a way of making large purchases that they normally could not afford otherwise. Debt is used by everyone, from considerable megacorporations to individuals. It comes in many different forms including various loans, lines of credit, and bills.

If you're not well-versed in using these types of debts, it's easy to see them as free money. However, all debts must be repaid, and the longer you take to pay them back, the more it will cost you. Debt accrues interest over time and, depending on your interest rate, the cost of any purchase can skyrocket substantially over a few months. Sure, having a credit card is helpful for when you need to make a purchase now and you don't get paid until next week, but it's easy to get carried away and start putting more than you can afford on your credit cards. When it comes time to pay the money back, you might find that you can't afford to do so, even if each purchase you made wasn't costly at all.

When misused, debt can become a force of destruction on your wallet, your lifestyle, and your ability to achieve your financial goals. However, when you take care to use debt in healthy ways, it can become a handy tool. To do so, you must understand the ins and outs of debt, starting with its many different forms.

TYPES OF DEBT

Not all debt is equal. Some debts can be more beneficial than others, helping you to achieve different life goals without excessively high interest rates. In contrast, others can interfere with your ability to pursue your objectives when they're mismanaged. Common types of debt include credit lines, loans, mortgages, medical bills, and debts related to the government, such as property and income taxes. In this book, we'll mainly cover credit and loans since these are the most likely to become drastic issues, but it helps to have a basic understanding of debt in all its forms.

Credit

Credit, speaking generally, is any transaction where you borrow money that you agree to pay back at a later date. More specifically, in terms of debt, credit cards make up a large portion of many peoples' debt woes. One reason credit cards can become such a big issue is due to a lack of credit literacy. Many people who sign up for credit cards just don't know how to use them effectively or they end up misunderstanding the terms of their card and spend too much without thinking about how they'll pay it back.

Credit card debt builds rapidly due to high interest rates and fees. If you don't pay at least the minimum balance on your cards every month, you'll have to pay a penalty on top of what you already owe. Even if you pay the minimum balance, whatever's left will continue to accrue interest over time. This means one poorly thought out purchase can become a huge problem that affects your credit for months or years.

Still, credit cards are a part of our everyday lives. They're used by people, young and old, to gradually pay off large purchases or as a tool for building their credit. While they can be misused, they can also be very effective when used properly, as you'll learn how to do throughout this book.

Loans

Most loans are used to pay for large purchases like homes and business start-up fees, which means they will take much longer to pay off than credit cards with much smaller credit limits. Loans are often a method for investing in your future, as they can help you fund necessary home repairs or allow you to attend college. For education loans, it's often with the expectation that you'll be able to make more money post-graduation and thus repay your debts. In practice, though, this doesn't always work out as planned.

There are many types of loans, which can range in both price and repayment periods. You might take out an auto loan to help pay for the purchase of your new car, or you might qualify for student loans through the government or a private lender to help pay for your education expenses. Since loans can be tens of thousands of dollars, they can rapidly get out of hand and become very difficult to pay off in a reasonable amount of time, especially if your credit isn't good enough for a low interest rate.

To reduce the risk of losing money, lenders may ask for collateral before giving you a loan, which is an asset the lender can repossess if you fail to pay them back. For example, the collateral for an auto loan is your car. Other loans, like student loans, don't require any associated collateral, but they're still essential to pay on time.

Mortgages

The process of becoming a homeowner doesn't end when you find your dream house. In most cases, you will need to finance this purchase. When you take out a mortgage, the property you buy becomes the collateral for the loan. If you can't make your payments on time, the bank may foreclose on your house. In foreclosure, the bank repossesses your home and sells it to new buyers to recover as much of the loan balance as possible. Therefore, paying your mortgage should take priority, as failing to do so means losing your home.

Since most mortgages are hundreds of thousands of dollars, you'll typically need to make a down payment on the house you purchase. This shows your mortgage lender that you have enough money in your savings and income to pay your mortgage each month. It also indicates that you're no longer shopping around, and you're serious about acquiring this home. However, in practice, emergencies and surprise bills can make keeping up with your mortgage payments more difficult than anticipated.

Medical Debt

Most US hospitals are required by law to provide life-saving care whether you have the means to pay for it or not. This is great when your life is in danger, but you will eventually have to pay the bill for your care. Medical debt can be anywhere from a few hundred dollars to a few hundred thousand depending on the type of care you receive, and while good health insurance can cover some of the cost, it rarely covers the whole bill.

Like other types of debt, medical debt can generate interest over time. If a procedure is incredibly costly, you might spend years trying to pay off a hospital bill long after the initial trip to the doctor's office. There is no collateral for medical debt as doctors can't "take back" the care they provided, but failing to pay these bills can still impact your credit.

Tax and Government Sources of Debt

You may not realize it at first, but taxes are another form of debt. Rather than owing money to a private lender, you owe your state and federal government. If you work for an employer, the government automatically takes a portion of each paycheck to pre-pay these taxes. If you work for yourself or you make money from various investments, you might pay them quarterly or in one sum for the year. Either way, any differences in what you owe and what you paid are resolved come tax season, and you'll either get a refund or a bill depending on if you over or underpaid.

It's easy to stay on top of tax debt when it's an automated process, but it can become an issue if you underestimate your payments or work for yourself and fail to save for tax day. Stay on top of filing your tax return and know how much you owe each year to minimize the risk of owing the government money. Unlike other debts, committing tax evasion is considered a crime and it can come with hefty fines or even jail time. This is one debt you most certainly want to avoid.

THE UGLY SIDE OF DEBT

On the surface, debt doesn't seem so bad. You borrow money, you eventually pay it back, and both you and the lender are happy. While this is ideally how each new loan or line of credit would work, in practice, things rarely go as smoothly.

Debt can become a huge problem, primarily if you rely on it too heavily. If your debt gets out of control, you could have mounting interest issues and maxing out your credit cards. This can lead to constantly stressing over your finances, ruining your credit score, and losing a large chunk of your income to paying off your debts.

Building Interest

High interest rates can multiply the amount of money you owe on any purchase. Let's say your fridge broke and you need to buy a new one. You can't afford one right now, so you put it on your credit card. You buy a $500 fridge using a credit card with a 20% interest rate. If you fail to pay off your purchase by the end of the year, that fridge has become $100 more expensive. Now, imagine you put multiple purchases on that credit card and you have trouble paying them off for months or even years. You're going to end up with debt that far outweighs the money you originally borrowed.

This gets even worse when you consider compound interest. Compounding interest means debt can build at an exponential rate, quickly becoming too much to handle. If you don't pay off your debt by the end of the compounding period, usually a month, you get charged interest on top of your accrued interest. In other words, the interest was calculated based on the $500 original cost. The next time it'll be calculated on the $600 you now owe, plus any fees from your cardholder. Most credit cards compound your interest daily.

The Danger of Available Credit Limits

Everybody wants a higher credit limit on their card, right? Sure, it might feel good to know you can put $2,000 worth of purchases on your credit card, but just because your credit limit is high doesn't mean you can afford to pay off that much money.

In fact, high credit limits can subconsciously encourage you to spend more than you should.

If your credit limit were only a few hundred dollars, there would be no temptation to overspend since you wouldn't be able to rack up debt. When your limit is far greater than your budget, you might keep spending until you max out the credit limit. Chances are you can't afford to pay all of it back at once, which means you'll owe interest and possibly penalty fees on the remainder.

Stress and Financial Woes

Debt is a huge contributor to stress for so many people because it can leave you feeling trapped and helpless. You might go about your day constantly thinking about how much you owe in the back of your mind. Constant rumination isn't suitable for anyone, especially if you don't have a clear plan of attack for dealing with all of the debt on your plate.

You may also feel stressed because your debt is keeping you from achieving your financial goals. If you want to move into a nicer house, buy that new car you've had your eye on, or provide for your family, but you can't afford to because of your debt, financial stress becomes a significant source of worry and regret. The only way to ease these woes is to dig yourself out of the hole.

Impact on Your Credit Score

Outstanding debt can tank your credit score. The more missed payments and maxed-out credit lines you have under your name, the worse your credit score will get. This is a huge problem because your credit score is what creditors use to determine how trustworthy you are and a low credit score can disqualify you from a lot of offers, which includes opening a new credit card, taking out a mortgage with a lower interest rate, financing a car, and applying to live in an apartment. Some employers may even check your credit score before offering you a job. A low credit score can also make it more difficult to consolidate your debt and refinance, making it even harder to pay off your debts.

Monopolizing Your Income

All of the debt you rack up each month needs to be paid down. Even if you're only making the minimum payments, it will start to eat into your paychecks. In some cases, your debt might even increase enough that you owe more each month than what you earn. This can make it nearly impossible to pay off your debt the usual way and still afford other bills and necessary purchases. When you no longer have disposable income thanks to high amounts of debt, you no longer have control over your finances.

IS DEBT ALWAYS BAD?

Debt can be a destructive force in your life, but does that mean it's always a bad thing? If it was, it's unlikely anyone would ever get a credit card or take out a loan. The truth is that debt can have positive or negative outcomes depending on how you use it. When debt is used to make extravagant purchases you don't need, without paying attention to the consequences of these purchases, it has negative repercussions. When you only borrow what you can pay back, and you use debt as a way to make worthwhile purchases as investments in your future, it can be a highly effective tool. Good debt lets you manage your finances more effectively. With good debt, you're able to leverage your wealth to prepare yourself for emergencies and buy things you actually need rather than buying from a perspective of pure want.

Mortgages are considered good debt. This is because they help you purchase a house, which will almost always cost more money than what you have in the bank unless you have saved for months or years. Additionally, the property is an investment, both financially and in terms of your safety and future. It isn't a wasteful purchase, even though it's an expensive one. Since mortgages are large long-term loans, they don't harm your credit score and their interest rates tend to be far lower than short-term loans and credit cards. As a result, you can borrow without significantly overpaying and your credit score won't suffer for it. In fact, the more on-time payments you make, the better your credit score will become. Of course, missing mortgage payments can hurt your credit, but this is true of any loan. If you make payments on time, your credit score won't be negatively affected.

Student loans are also considered good debt. While they can be challenging to pay off, they grant you the opportunity to go to school and get a degree you wouldn't have been able to afford otherwise. Your degree can qualify you for higher-paying jobs, which ideally should make paying off the loans more manageable. You can also get help from the government if you struggle to repay your loans. For example, many government-subsidized loans don't require you to pay interest until after you graduate. People with low income may qualify for deferred or income-driven repayment plans, which ensures your debt doesn't exceed your paycheck.

Mortgages and student loans are debts worth taking out, but you'll still need to stick to a repayment schedule. Debt can be a force for good, but only if you use it responsibly.

WHERE TO GET LOANS

Whether you need to cover tuition for your next semester at college or you want to fund your new business venture, you'll need to get a loan. Each financial institution that offers loans, including banks, credit unions, and peer-to-peer lenders, has different rules and average loan rates. Consider the option that is best for your circumstances before taking out a loan of any kind.

Banks

Banks are one of the most convenient options for obtaining a personal loan. Most chain banks have local branches all across the nation, which means that you can apply for a loan in person as well as online. This means you can access resources such as a credit specialist, who can help you look at your options and choose the best loan for your situation. They can also guide you through the application, payout, and repayment processes.

Banks are a great option if you have good credit and you're looking to pay off your debt before it becomes a bigger problem, but they might not be the right fit if you're already having credit issues. For one, banks are well-funded, so they can afford to be picky about whom they lend to. Most have a strict set of rules about who does and doesn't qualify for a loan, and if your credit is poor, you may not make the list. If you do, you might end up paying more in interest than you would from other lenders. Bank loans may have interest rates as low as 5-6%, but they may also be as high as 25%.

Credit Unions

Credit unions are typically more exclusive than banks. You'll need to be a member to use their services, though this may be as simple as filling out an application. They also serve smaller areas than most banks and may not be available locally, depending on where you live. However, credit unions typically offer far better repayment options and interest rates than banks if you have access to them. You may also qualify for loans even if you have subpar credit, which may be more beneficial for you as a borrower since credit unions aren't as focused on turning a profit as banks are. Still, the credit unions with the best rates tend to be very selective about their membership requirements. Most credit unions only need to know that you're employed, but some require you to work in specific professions such as education or government work. Some credit unions may even require that you are referred by a current member. Check the membership requirements of any credit union before trying to apply for a personal loan.

Peer-to-Peer Lenders

Peer-to-peer (P2P) lending is a type of loan given by another individual. As someone who has worked at two major P2P lenders, I firmly believe in their business model, which connects ordinary people with lenders who know what it's like to be an average person struggling with debt. Lenders get repaid with interest over time and you're able to enjoy the knowledge that any interest you pay isn't going to some nameless, faceless executive, but another person.

Each P2P lending company and website has different qualification requirements. As a whole, they tend to be more lenient than banks and credit unions while also having lower interest rates, but there are some exceptions. Do your research before choosing to work with any P2P lending companies, but don't disregard this unique personal loan source. Someday when you've escaped debt and achieved financial stability, you may even be able to return the favor and become a P2P lender yourself.

UNDERSTANDING APR AND INTEREST RATES

Before taking out a loan or opening a credit line, you need to have a solid understanding of annual percentage rates (APRs) and interest rates. Without this knowledge, you're far more likely to end up in tons of debt. While APR and interest rates both refer to how interest accrues on your loans over time, they're not exact synonyms. Knowing the difference can help you better compare different lenders' rates and avoid getting blindsided by interest.

Interest Rate

The interest rate seems like the most important consideration when comparing loans, but it can be deceptive. It doesn't tell you as much about the loan's terms as you might think. An interest rate is a percentage of the principal loan balance and does not include any fees that you might incur with the loan. Remember that most loan balances are calculated using compound interest, which isn't accounted for in the interest rate. Unlike the APR, it doesn't include other fees the lender might apply to your account, so it can be somewhat deceptive.

These can include origination or loan processing fees, underwriting fees charged for evaluating your loan application, and document preparation fees. You may also be charged with an escrow fee if you're taking out a mortgage, which pays the third party company holding your deposit until the loan is approved or denied.

APR

Like interest rates, a loan's APR is also a measure of interest you'll have to pay on the initial loan balance. The APR is typically higher than the interest rate, but it's also a more accurate look at how much you'll be paying each year. Unlike the interest rate, a loan's APR includes all associated fees you can expect to pay on your principal, assuming you don't have any penalties. It accounts for any mortgage insurance premiums, brokerage fees, and loan origination fees, and it deducts any mortgage points if your loan includes them.

If you're trying to compare two different loans purely price-wise, the APR is a more reliable measure of how much the loan will cost you than the interest rate alone. Look for lower APRs, but also consider other factors like the level of service or the flexibility of the offered repayment plans. When you consider all factors carefully, you'll know what to expect from each loan you take out, enabling you to use debt to your advantage.

2

MOUNTAINS OF CREDIT CARD INTEREST

"The real joy in life comes from finding your true purpose and aligning it with what you do every single day."

— TONY ROBBINS

Interest can be devastating if you let it continue to grow over time. Every time you make a partial payment on your credit cards or you miss a payment entirely, your interest accrues. You likely already know just how bad this can be from experience and yet it's still difficult to keep yourself from spending more than you can afford. Once you've built up mountains of interest, it's even harder to pay your balance off entirely, which makes it easier to get into the habit of having to rely on your credit cards.

If interest is such a big problem, why do so many people continue to use their credit cards in irresponsible ways? Part of the reason is because of the subtle ways having a credit card can influence you to misuse it. It's easy to make mistakes and misuse your credit cards, landing yourself in hot water, especially if you tend to buy things you don't need as a form of "retail therapy" or to keep up with the latest fashion and tech trends. Understanding these pressures can help you navigate them without giving in so you can develop a healthy relationship with credit and kick debt to the curb. Once you know what not to do, you'll stop making your debt problems bigger. Then you can start paying off your more manageable amount of debt.

EASE OF CREDIT CARD USE

Credit cards are so popular because of their convenience. For one, it's often easier to hand over a piece of plastic or read off a card number than to make purchases with cash or checks, but this is true of debit cards as well. What makes credit cards so convenient and easily misused is how they let you defer payments to a later date, which encourages excessive spending.

You don't have to have money to spend with a credit card. In fact, with large credit limits, you can rack up a lot of debt. The higher your credit limit is, the more you're encouraged to spend, even though this is a poor way to maintain a healthy relationship with your credit. It's effortless to rely on your credit card, especially when you're in a tight spot financially, and you can't afford to buy something otherwise, but it can be tough to pay these purchases off later.

Additionally, significant credit limits can make it very easy to lose track of how much you're spending. Sometimes credit card debt comes from a single large purchase, but it's usually the unfortunate outcome of making many small purchases that add up over time. When you make a single big purchase, you know exactly how much you're spending, but with a large credit limit, you might continue to make small purchases without realizing the amount you're actually spending. The total of your small purchases could exceed what you would have spent on something expensive without stopping to ask yourself if you need them, which leads to large amounts of debt.

Credit issues can be exacerbated by many other factors that make credit cards a more appealing option than other forms of payment. For example, if you have very little in your savings account and you need an emergency car repair, the only way you can afford to pay for it is with a credit card. At times, it can be harder to save money than it is to use a credit card, even if the credit card will end up being more of a nuisance later on. Excess spending in general, whether motivated by a desire to buy the newest flashy piece of technology or just not knowing how to keep a budget, is a vast contributor to credit card debt.

Credit cards may also entice you into spending more with flashy deals that look great on the surface but require you to spend money you can't afford to repay. When you get into a tight spot, want to buy something just to impress your friends or have to spend a certain amount to get cashback, simply reaching for your credit card quickly becomes a habit that's almost impossible to break if you don't recognize how damaging it could be.

MARKETING AND SOCIAL ACCEPTANCE

Overspending is one of the driving forces of credit card debt. You buy too much without any concern for how you're going to pay it off. But why do so many people overspend, especially on unnecessary purchases? This is often the result of social pressures that encourage you to 'keep up with the Joneses'—or, in more modern terms, you experience the fear of missing out (FOMO) that comes when your friends and neighbors have things you can't afford.

We are constantly surrounded by advertisements and other marketing materials suggesting how much better our lives would be if we had bought a particular product. Ads are intended to capture our attention and convince us that we can't live without their products, so they're hard to ignore by design. Making us believe that the product is more important than figuring out how to pay for it subtly influences us to use any means available to make the purchase, especially credit cards. A car commercial promises you'll turn heads if you buy this new pricey vehicle instead of an older but affordable model. A magazine ad shows how expensive clothes can score you a date or help you net your dream job. You'll be totally missing out if you don't buy the latest model iPhone. Products become a vehicle for social acceptance and holding up the status quo. These advertisements all have the same conclusion: buying these things will make you happy, so you should spend more money. If you don't have enough money in your bank account, your FOMO might drive you to use your credit cards instead.

Credit Card Marketing

Ads for products of any kind can be misleading, including advertisements for credit cards themselves. Lenders might promise phenomenal benefits and few fees, but when you sign up for the card, you quickly find out that these promises weren't what they seemed on the surface. Many credit card companies have gotten themselves in hot water for purposefully misleading customers and encouraging bad borrowing practices to increase their profits. In 2012, Discover was successfully sued by customers who were misled by call center operators to sign up for free payment/wallet protection, credit score tracking, and identity theft protection. These products and services were in no way free of charge and Discover then billed these customers. A similar penalty was levied against American Express the same year which misled consumers about the initial bonuses they would receive for signing up for certain credit cards after meeting certain qualifications. These qualifications generally entail spending $3,000 or more in the first 3 months and receiving $300 cash back or in bonuses, which causes you to potentially feel the need to spend more than what you can pay off in order to get the bonus. This doesn't mean you shouldn't get a credit card, but be aware that deceptive marketing can lead you to misuse or overuse if you don't fully understand their terms and conditions.

To avoid this:

1. Try to get all promises in writing so you can refer back to those documents if needed. You can double check the exact terms of your card. Remember, credit issuers are less likely to lie in writing than they would be over the phone.
2. Read any information you get about a card carefully, especially if you have to sign off on it.
3. Track and review your monthly statements for accuracy.

If you see any suspicious charges, contact your lender right away. The sooner you notice a problem, the easier it is to correct it, which increases your chances of getting your money back.

It's important to evaluate any financial move carefully and to consider whether you need it or not. This goes for both the products you purchase as well as the cards you use to buy them. Marketing can prey on your FOMO and get you to do things without thinking them through. The more attuned you are to the problems that lead to misusing credit cards, the less trouble you will have avoiding them.

SHOULD YOU CANCEL A CREDIT CARD?

The standard advice for avoiding the accumulation of credit card interest dictates that you should cancel your credit cards, but is this really the best course of action? The truth is a little less clear-cut. While canceling a card can help lower your overall spending limit so that you're less tempted to make unnecessary purchases, there are plenty of reasons to keep cards around, too. It's better to learn how to use them responsibly rather than trying to stop using credit altogether. Still, there are some situations where limiting the number of cards you have can help you get your spending under control.

Ultimately, the decision of whether or not you should cancel a card depends on several factors. Consider how often you use the card and how old the card is, both of which can impact your spending habits and your credit score.

Frequency of Use

How often you use your credit card can be a big determining factor in whether or not you should cancel it. If you get a lot of use out of your card, it's probably not a good idea to cancel it, but this can also mean you're overusing your card. Here are some important considerations to make before you make any move to cancel.

First, how much debt have you accumulated on the card? In most cases, you'll need to pay off all your debt before you can close out that line of credit. If you have a very high balance, it might be a while before you could reasonably pay it off, even if the high balance suggests it's a card you might use too frequently. Since you can't cancel the card yet, it would be beneficial to stop using it and resolve to pay down your balance before you make any more purchases with it. Many credit card companies will allow you to put a hold on the card, so you can't authorize new payments until you get the card unfrozen. This is a great way to cut down on card usage without closing the account.

Some credit card companies charge an annual fee for having the card, whether you use it or not. This is typical for cards with good sign-on and cashback bonuses. Unlike penalty fees, it's impossible to avoid paying an annual fee unless you cancel the card completely. Therefore, you may want to cancel these cards if you're not using them often enough to benefit from the cashback bonuses.

You'll have to balance this consideration with the effect that your credit limit has on your credit score. Your score is affected by your credit utilization, which is the ratio of the credit available to you across all of your accounts versus the amount you're currently using. Having a higher available credit limit can benefit your score, but only if you don't use it all. It might be worth keeping a card around that you infrequently use just to keep your credit utilization healthy. However, if this high credit limit only encourages you to spend, consider leaving the card in a desk drawer to eliminate this temptation.

Finally, remember to check your card activity often so you can detect fraud as soon as possible. If you're not frequently using a card, you probably won't scrutinize its balance consistently, which means you might not notice someone else is using your card until they've racked up a lot of debt under your name. This is an incredibly massive concern if you don't get purchase notifications or automatic statements. If you're going to keep an unused or infrequently used card open, check on it every couple of months. If you think you won't remember to do so, you might be better off closing the account.

Age of the Card

Your credit can be impacted by your card's age. The older your credit history is, the better this reflects on you as a borrower. If you don't have a lot of history, lenders don't have a lot of data regarding your habits as a borrower. If you close a very old card, especially one that you got when you first started using credit, you shorten your credit history. This can negatively impact your credit score and you might look more inexperienced in the eyes of a lender.

The older a card is, the more hesitant you should be to close it. This seems counterproductive, as your old cards might have worse terms and interest rates than newer ones. Still, it might be worth keeping your oldest credit card around even if you don't use it anymore and occasionally make payments on it to keep it from going inactive so that you don't harm your credit score. You might choose to pay a utility bill with the card and set it up to pay its balance off automatically, so you don't have to constantly check in on it while enjoying the benefits that a more extensive credit history provides. Closing an old card is less of an issue if you have multiple cards that are equally old. Suppose you've been borrowing for a long time. In that case, your credit history's length is typically a less critical factor in determining your credit score than payment history or credit utilization.

Either way, you can typically close new cards without the hassle. Let's say you got a card a few months ago to take advantage of its sign-on bonus, but you haven't used it much since. This card doesn't contribute to your credit history's age so you can cancel it safely. When a card is older, you should consider this decision carefully and weigh it against your overall credit health. If you only have one card, keep it open so you don't lose your entire credit history.

STOP CHARGING ON YOUR CREDIT CARD!

The first step towards paying off your credit cards is to stop using them. This doesn't mean you can't ever use credit again. It just means that the more you continue to spend, the more debt accumulates, and the harder it becomes to pay your debt off. You can give yourself a debt reset by halting new purchases as often as possible so that each payment you make has a more significant impact on the amount you owe. Once you quit spending and pay down the balance, you can decide whether or not you want to use credit cards again and start with a clean slate.

Breaking the Credit Card Habit

Quitting credit card use, even if only for a short while, requires you to break free of the bad habits you've gotten used to. You may need to resort to some creative approaches to accomplish this. For example, you could keep your cards out of sight and leave them in a desk drawer or lockbox, making it more difficult for you to get to them. Even just leaving cards you're not planning on using at home when you want to curb your spending can be enough of a barrier to keep you from making impulse purchases.

You may also be able to reason your way out of excessive spending if you take a moment to recognize how much it's affecting you. Sit down and make a list of everything you owe on each of your accounts. Then, go to https:// allenanything.com to use my online debt repayment calculator included in the free workbook to see how long it will take to pay off your debt and determine how much more you'll need to pay to reach your debt-free date. Repayment may take anywhere from a few months to a few years—assuming you don't make any more purchases in that time. This is a great way to jumpstart better spending habits, as you can see in plain terms just how much of a problem credit card debt can be.

Don't forget to use milestone markers and rewards to pat yourself on the back when you successfully improve your credit habits. Tell yourself you'll only play your favorite video game on days when you refrain from buying something on a credit card. When you pay back a certain percentage of your outstanding credit card debt, celebrate your achievement in a way that doesn't make you take on more debt, like going out to eat with money you've saved up. This can replace the rush of happiness that retail therapy provides and keep you on the right track to eliminate excessive spending.

What About Automatic Payments?

It's possible that you're not yet financially stable enough to stop using your credit cards altogether; you might use your credit cards for various automatic payments, so you can't cancel them all at once. While it's not always easy to stop making impulse purchases, it's even harder to quit using credit cards when you're already in the habit of using them to pay your bills. While this can be a slippery slope, it's not necessarily a bad thing to use credit cards for recurring payments like your car insurance or electric bill, as long as you don't let debt linger on these cards for too long.

The best rule of thumb for setting up automatic payments is that you should be able to pay more than the minimum balance each billing period. Each payment will help you reduce your outstanding balance and considerably cut down on the amount of interest you owe, so one month's bill won't become an expense that sticks around for multiple years. Ideally, you should be able to pay off each bill in a month or two to keep debt from accumulating; as long as you contribute more than the minimum monthly payment, you're headed in the right direction.

Once you've stopped paying for unnecessary purchases with credit, you can shift your focus to lowering your balance and avoiding delinquency.

3

DELINQUENCY DILEMMAS

"By asking the question 'How can I afford it?' your brain is put to work."

— ROBERT KIYOSAKI

Making late payments or missing payments interferes with your ability to get your debt back under control. Not only will you incur additional fees that increase how much you owe, but it's also bad for your credit. Consistently making payments on time is the most significant factor in determining your credit score. Even if you have issues in other areas like your credit usage or your accounts' age, you can keep your score reasonably high if you make at least the minimum payment for each line of credit you have open. Of course, it's better to pay more if you can, but at the very least, you should strive to make payments on time each month. Otherwise, your credit will take a huge hit with each late payment, which can make it much harder to qualify for reasonable interest rates and consolidation of your debts for easier repayment.

When you miss a payment, your account is considered delinquent even if you are only late by one day. Delinquent accounts are subject to many different fees, and these will only accumulate the more prolonged the debt goes unpaid. If you're delinquent on multiple payments, your lender may even freeze your account until you've repaid some or all of what you owe. This can be a big problem if you use a credit card to pay a bill or make another necessary purchase. They can also employ various measures to essentially force you to pay off your debt, all of which can cause you more problems than if you had simply stuck to making payments on your own terms. These include sending your debt to collections, taking legal action against you, repossessing the collateral for a loan, and in some cases garnishing your wages.

Luckily, the trick to avoiding delinquency is straightforward: make payments on time. Avoid spending so much that you can't afford to make the minimum payment. If this does happen, discuss solutions with your lender rather than letting the debt go unpaid; otherwise, you'll need to deal with debt collectors and other troubles that come with delinquent accounts.

DEBT COLLECTORS

Debt collectors are sort of like bounty hunters. Their job is to get you to pay what you owe by any means available to them. They may work for the lender that initially issued you your credit line, taking a percentage of what you owe for their services, or they may be a separate company that essentially purchases your debt from the original creditor. Either way, their payment depends on their ability to get you to pay, so many debt collectors have earned a reputation for being somewhat aggressive. While there are regulations in place to protect you from unfair collection practices, it's important to know all the tricks collectors have available to them, so you know what to expect if you fail to make payments on time. Typically, you won't end up in a debt collector's crosshairs if you miss just one or two payments, but if you let the missed payments stack up, they're sure to set their sights on you sooner or later.

Debt collectors usually get involved after a loan enters default, which means you've failed to meet the repayment terms of the agreement you made when you borrowed the money. Loans move from delinquency to default in a matter of weeks or months, depending on your lender's terms and standard practices. Most lenders will give you some time to correct the issue, but if they aren't paid what they're owed, they will eventually turn to debt collectors. Any source of overdue payments on a credit card balance, such as phone bills, auto loan payments, utility bills, back taxes, etc. and your debt will be turned over to a collections agency or debt collector generally within three to six months of default. Once your debt passes into a collector's hands, they'll take over the work of tracking you down and getting you to pay what you owe.

Dealing with debt collectors can look a little different depending on whether they're part of an in-house collections department or a separate collection agency. Learn who is responsible for collecting your debt first and foremost—you should receive a letter or email any time your debt changes hands. This way, you know what to expect, and you can be sure you're repaying the right person after you default on a loan. Oftentimes, this is different than how you would have previously made payments. You don't want to find out you've been sending money to the wrong company for months. Remember that all lenders and collection agencies are responsible for managing hundreds of accounts, so they might not notice payments have been going to the wrong person for a while. Ultimately, you must keep track of your debts yourself, so you know where your money is going, but careful tracking can only get you so far. You must also pay off these debts and report any credit errors so they can be corrected.

In-House Collections Departments

An in-house collections department is part of the same company as your loan issuer. For example, if you have a credit card with Discover and they have their own collections department, you'll speak to someone who works for Discover. This is also called a first-party debt collector. Typically, in-house collectors will respond to delinquent debts faster than if the lender has to sell the debt to a collection agency. They're more common among large companies that can afford to have their own dedicated department.

There are some notable advantages to working with a first-party debt collector. Even though your account might be in collections, this doesn't necessarily mean your lender wants you to close your account. Many in-house collectors are instructed to try and keep you as a customer while working with you to repay your debts so that you may have access to more lenient terms and extended repayment periods. They may also be willing to forgive a portion of your debt if they think it will keep you from closing your account. Typically, they will use less aggressive methods, but keep in mind they still have access to all of the same strategies as other collectors and may use them if necessary.

Collection Agencies

Collection agencies allow lenders to outsource the collection process. Essentially, your lender sells your debt for a fraction of what it's worth to a debt collector, who in turn tries to collect the full amount—or as much as they can get. They profit when you repay them and lose out when you don't, and since this is the primary way these companies make money, they're often much more dependent on you paying them. This means they're more likely to use extreme methods without having to worry about whether you want to keep your credit line open since they weren't the ones who issued it in the first place. They also have more time and resources to pursue your debt with, so they're less likely to decide it's not worth the trouble and write it off, even if you don't owe very much.

What Collectors Are and Aren't Allowed to Do

When you think "debt collector," you might have a mental picture of a muscly enforcer standing outside your home with a crowbar. Luckily, collectors aren't allowed to do anything like this in real life, but they can still use methods that range from mildly troublesome to very intrusive. You'll typically be notified by letter or phone call first, but debt collectors will take more and more extreme measures if the debt goes unpaid. They can call not only your home and cell phone but your work phone too. They may show up at your home or contact your friends and family to get updated contact information about you as well. If you continue to fail to repay your debt, having an account in collections will negatively impact your credit score for up to seven years.

While collectors might employ all of these tactics to pressure you into paying back your debt, you have certain rights and protections afforded to you by the Fair Debt Collection Practices Act and the Federal Trade Commission (FTC). Debt collectors are prohibited from using abusive, unfair, or deceptive practices during the debt collection process. For example, while collectors can contact your family to ask about your whereabouts, they are not allowed to disclose why they need that information. You can also limit the amount of harassment you receive from collectors with a cease and desist letter if they contact you repeatedly. Collectors can't try to contact you outside of reasonable hours, so you shouldn't get any calls before 8:00 a.m. or after 9:00 p.m. They also cannot threaten you with physical harm, nor can they lie about the consequences of not paying back your loan. You cannot go to jail for failing to pay back a debt either. There are some cases where you might have your property repossessed, but the collector needs to win a lawsuit against you first, so you won't ever end up without your car or house without any warning.

These regulations are meant to protect you. While it's best to pay off your debts long before entering the collections stage, debt collectors must treat you fairly and adhere to these guidelines so you shouldn't feel bullied or threatened by them. Collector regulations also give you the power to dispute issues and errors that misrepresent how much you owe.

HOW TO DISPUTE CREDIT

Accidents and oversights happen, even in financial matters. If you get a bill you don't recognize or if something on your credit report doesn't look right, be sure to dispute it by following the proper channels. Suppose a charge is successfully disputed because it's fraudulent or was recorded incorrectly. In that case, you won't have to pay for the part of the bill that was made in error, and it will no longer negatively impact your credit. The same is true of any mistakes in your credit report, whether they're the result of malicious intent or pure human error.

Checking your statements and your free credit report routinely can help you identify and dispute any errors before they turn into delinquencies for debts you don't actually owe. Make sure you're only paying for the purchases you've really made, which you can do by comparing your receipts to your credit card bills. If you notice a discrepancy, dispute it as soon as possible.

Disputing Credit Card Billing Errors

If you don't recognize a purchase on your credit card, quick action on your part can keep you from getting stuck with the bill. First, make sure the charge is fraudulent. If any family members or friends have access to your card or any online accounts that might store your card information, it's possible that they may have made the purchase. If it doesn't sound familiar to anyone you know, then you can report it. Federal law states that you cannot be held liable for more than $50 in fraudulent charges, no matter how large the purchase is. However, most lenders won't hold you responsible for the disputed charge as long as you report it in a timely manner. Ideally, you should alert your credit card company within two billing cycles so they can look into the issue. If you overlook the case within this timeframe, you may still be held responsible for paying the fraudulent bill.

There are many reasons why you might need to dispute a charge on your credit card and not all of them are the result of some shadowy figure committing fraud. A clerical error might have added an extra zero to the end of an otherwise legitimate charge. You might dispute a charge if the product or service you received didn't match up to what the seller promised and you refused it. Your credit card company might not have recorded a payment you made or accounted for a merchandise return. Even a statement listing the wrong date for something you bought is important to correct, as this can affect the billing period the purchase falls under.

Some credit card companies allow you to dispute fraudulent charges online or over the phone, but the most reliable method is always through the mail. Even if it takes longer this way, using certified mail means you get a verification the letter was delivered, creating a paper trail that proves you took action and the fraudulent charge cannot be held against you. The FTC provides sample letters for disputing each type of billing error on their website. Send the credit card company the appropriate letter informing them of the error and you should get a response within a month. Many creditors will temporarily write off the charge while they look into the issue, though it can be added back to your account if they discover it's not fraud after all. The process is a little different if you're disputing a charge on the basis of not receiving the service you paid for or if there was a billing error. You should first ask the seller for a replacement or refund. If they refuse, keep any documentation of your attempt and notify your credit card company immediately.

Disputing Credit Score Reporting Errors

Is your credit report accurate? Maybe you've never thought to ask this question before. This wouldn't be surprising, given that most people tend to assume credit bureaus have everything figured out. In reality, errors on your credit report are much more common than you'd think. A 2012 study by the FTC found that approximately 25% of US consumers discovered errors that could affect their credit scores in one of their credit reports. These can be as small and easily remedied as an incorrect credit limit or balance that hasn't been updated or as significant as having your credit information mixed up with a total stranger's credit history. Make sure your name, phone number, and address are all correct and up to date, as something as minor as a wrong keystroke could make it difficult for lenders to look up your credit report successfully. Unfortunately, many people don't look for these errors, so they don't realize how this impacts their credit score. Once a year, you can request a copy of your credit report from all three major credit bureaus for free and it's a good idea to make sure those reports from Equifax, TransUnion, and Experian all match up.

If you do find an error, your first step should be to inform the relevant credit bureaus. You can do this through the mail or online at each bureau's website. The Consumer Financial Protection Bureau (CFPB) has templates you can use for your letter on their website. It's also a good idea to contact whichever company provided the incorrect information to the credit bureau if you know it. For example, if there's an issue related to one of your credit cards, let that lender know about the problem so they can correct it on their end, too. Once your letter is received, credit bureaus have thirty days to investigate and another five to report their findings back to you, after which you can dispute their investigation results further if they're still inaccurate. If the issue is fixed, it may take a few months before it displays correctly on your credit report, so don't be worried if it doesn't appear to be resolved right away.

WHAT HAPPENS WHEN YOU DISPUTE

So, you've tracked down errors on your credit card bill or credit report, compiled your proof, and shipped all this off for review. What's next? Sending in a credit dispute isn't the end of the story for you or the lender receiving your claim. For their part, the lender is then responsible for performing an investigation, recording their results, communicating these results to you, and making any necessary changes if they agree that an error has been made. Sometimes, however, they might disagree and push back against your attempt to correct a mistake, especially if you don't follow the dispute process to a T. It's crucial to know your rights as a borrower so you can come out on top of these disagreements.

Let's take a closer look at this process, so you know what to do if you end up locked in a battle of wills with a credit bureau.

Investigation

After the credit bureau receives your letter, they have 30 days to complete their investigation. If you send additional information after the initial letter, this timeframe increases by another 15 days to look into the issue. During this time, the credit bureau will reach out and notify the lender or other business that supplied the incorrect information, also known as the credit furnisher. Once the furnisher has all the necessary documents, they will perform their investigation to verify your claim's validity. Suppose they agree there's an error that needs to be corrected. In that case, they will automatically send this information to all three credit bureaus, so there's no need to contact each one individually unless they don't update your information.

Results and Credit Updates

During this stage, you'll hear back from the credit bureau and furnisher with their positive or negative investigation findings and you'll likely either celebrate or throw the report down in frustration. Ideally, you'll get a response notifying you that the error has been looked into and corrected. You'll get a new credit report with the correct adjustment made about 30 days after the dispute is resolved. If something was inaccurate or unverified, it will either no longer be on your report, or the false information will be adjusted. However, just because you get a new copy of your credit report doesn't always mean the error was fixed—read the report carefully, and make sure it's different from the one they sent you previously. If not, you may have to dispute the results of their investigation further.

In less ideal circumstances, the credit bureau might not correct the information. They may say they were unable to verify the incorrect information, which means they either didn't investigate to their full capabilities or they didn't have access to the necessary documentation to prove your claim. They may inform you that the documents you sent are unacceptable or illegible, in which case you should review them for accuracy and resubmit if necessary. In some cases, they may refuse to investigate because they've decided your error report is 'frivolous,' which typically means they believe your claims are incorrect. Essentially, you're trying to dispute too many things. If this happens, they will also send information about how to restart the investigation. If you get no response after about 45 days from when you first sent the dispute, you can resend the letter, as by law, they are required to look into it and inform you of their findings.

How to Dispute the Investigation Results

If the investigation results aren't in line with what you know to be true, you still have some options available. First, get in contact with the furnisher rather than the credit bureau. Supply them with evidence of your claims and make sure someone with access to your credit records is looking into the issue. You may also need to go directly to your lender if the mistake comes from their database or an error in their software, which is likely affecting many of their customers, not just you.

Sometimes credit bureaus won't give your dispute its due diligence. You have options for recourse for this, too. You can submit a statement of about 100 words pointing out the error in question that will be included each time someone checks your credit. Suppose you feel your borrower's rights have been violated and the credit bureau hasn't fully complied with the law. In that case, you can take legal action, either by notifying the CFPB of your complaint or by speaking to a consumer rights attorney about a lawsuit. Keep in mind that these lawsuits can get expensive, but a good lawyer will help you understand whether or not you have a worthwhile case.

WHEN DEBT IS WRITTEN OFF

Wouldn't it be nice to have your debts wiped clean? As great as this would be, the reality of debt being written off is a little more complicated. First of all, this typically only becomes a possibility if it's been a few years since you borrowed the money and you haven't been able to repay it since then. Creditors may instead accept a partial payment and, in exchange for getting some of their money back, write off the remainder. You'll need to work this out directly with your lender or debt collector.

On the other hand, if you don't work out a partial repayment and your lender simply informs you the debt has been written off, you may still have to pay for it. Writing off debt doesn't necessarily mean it's been forgiven, and it can still cause issues for you. For one, write-offs negatively impact your credit score. It's also possible the company might have sold your debt to a collections agency instead, which means you'll still be asked to pay what you owe and you may even have to pay additional interest.

How can you tell if you still owe the balance of your loan? By default, you should assume that debt getting written off doesn't mean it's been forgiven unless you are expressly notified of this by your lender, who will say the debt has been settled. If you receive a 1099-C "forgiven debt" form, your debt has been erased. Otherwise, there's a good chance you still need to pay.

Statute of Limitations

If you don't work in a legal field, about the only time you've heard the phrase "statute of limitations" is when you're watching a courtroom drama, but they can apply to many crimes that aren't nearly flashy enough to be on TV. The statute of limitations for any illegal act is the period of time during which you can have legal action taken against you. Each state has different laws regarding the statute of limitations for debt. It's typically "between three and six years, although in four states it's seven or more years" (Foreman, 2012, para. 8). Again, this doesn't necessarily mean that once you've surpassed the statute of limitations, the debt no longer exists. It just means you cannot be sued for the money you owe and a judge can't grant your lender the right to garnish your wages or otherwise take money from you without your consent. However, there's a good chance the collection agency will continue to contact you about your outstanding debt, even if they can't take you to court over it.

WILL DEBT COLLECTORS GIVE UP?

If you simply wait long enough, will your debts go away? The short answer is no, except in some fringe cases that involve decades of failed repayment. Waiting isn't your best course of action as each month that goes by where your debt remains unpaid is another month where your credit score is negatively impacted. Even if you're willing to put up with the hit to your credit, it's still probably not a good idea to just turn a blind eye to your debts and hope they go away.

As mentioned, the statute of limitations in regards to debt in your state means there's a hard limit on the amount of time you are legally liable to repay a debt, but just because you can't be sued doesn't mean the debt goes away at the end of that period. Additionally, even if your original lender gives up on your debt, they can still sell it to a collection agency that will soon come looking for what you owe. It is very rare for debts to be completely forgiven, especially if you avoid discussing them with your lenders. The only fool-proof way to resolve your debts is to create a repayment plan, work with your lender, and use other resources available to you, like consolidation and negotiation.

4

UNDERSTANDING GRACE

"Time is key to building your financial security."

— SUZE ORMAN

A s the old saying goes, time is money. This is just as true for paying off your credit cards and other types of debts as it is for many different areas of your life. If you delay making payments on your card, you'll end up owing more money thanks to interest and penalty fees. Mismanaging your time can cost you a lot of money. Luckily, the opposite is also true. If you leverage your time well and you take care to make punctual payments, you can save yourself plenty of money instead. Part of leveraging your time is understanding your credit card's grace period and how it can help you avoid accruing interest on your debts.

You don't need to pay your credit card bill the day you get it. It would be impossible for your lender to mail out a monthly statement and have it arrive at your door the same day, and you certainly couldn't complete a payment by mail within the same day either. Even though many buyers get their bills electronically, either through email or on a cell phone app linked to their credit cards, lenders don't expect you to pay them back the second you find out how much you owe. Online payments may take a few days to process and unforeseen emergencies can get in the way of making those payments. To account for possible delays, lenders set grace periods.

WHAT IS A GRACE PERIOD?

During the grace period, you won't be charged any interest or fines for not making a payment toward your debt. For credit cards, your grace period lasts from the end of the card's billing cycle, also known as the closing date, to the due date of your next payment. This typically lasts between a few weeks and a month. If your credit issuer offers a grace period, by law, your credit card statement must be made available to you no later than 21 days before the due date so you have at least three weeks to make your payment. Some companies may offer longer grace periods. Check your card's policy to see exactly how long you have before payment is due. Also, pay attention to what day your payment must be posted by so you're never late on a payment.

No interest is charged during the grace period if you can pay off the balance by the due date. If you make only the minimum payment or another amount less than the card's total debt, you'll be charged interest on the remainder. If you make no payment, you'll accrue interest plus any applicable penalty fees. Therefore, if you're making monthly payments during the grace period and paying off the full balance of the previous billing cycle, you are essentially taking advantage of a free loan while also improving your credit. However, if you don't pay the full balance, you end up on the hook for the interest and you might even lose your grace period.

Losing Your Grace Period

For most credit cards, grace periods are only available if you routinely make complete payments on time without issue. If you frequently make late or partial payments, your lender may take away your grace period. In addition to having to pay interest on the previous month's purchases, you'll also start accruing interest on new purchases right after you make them. This can significantly increase how much interest you owe, making it more expensive to pay back any purchases you make in the future. Since interest is applied automatically, you'll always be paying more for what you buy than if you hadn't used credit. This might not be a big issue if you don't owe much, but when you have thousands of dollars of credit card debt, this interest can really add up.

You'll likely lose your grace period for the entire time your credit card has a balance on it. All purchases will be more expensive when you put them on your credit card and using a card with a high interest rate can become a big problem. However, if you pay off your balance and practice good credit habits, you will be able to regain your grace period. You must demonstrate to your lender that you can keep up with payments again—which usually means paying the entire balance for at least two or three payment periods in a row. However, the exact policies of each credit card company may vary.

In short, if you want to get the greatest benefit from the grace period, you must only make as many purchases as you can afford to pay back at the end of the billing cycle. This is the best way to ensure you will always make full balance payments on time so you won't lose your grace period. It also eliminates the issue of interest, as you won't accrue any if you pay everything back on time. This doesn't mean there's no reason to use credit cards at all, of course. There's always the benefit of improving your credit over time with consistent good payment habits. Additionally, even if you always pay your balance in full, you can still delay payments for a few weeks if you put them on a credit card. This can give you just enough time to cash your next paycheck or recover from the latest financial emergency. When you use your grace period to your advantage, you can extend this time even further, leveraging your time wisely to avoid the pitfalls of interest.

AVOID INTEREST WITH GRACE

You might only have 21 days between when your billing period ends and when your payment is due, but this doesn't mean you have to pay off every purchase precisely 21 days after you make it. Any purchases made within the billing period, whether you make them on the first day or the last day, share the same grace period. This means that if you're smart about when you spend your money, you can maximize the amount of time between charging your card and paying for it.

To see how this plays out, let's look at an example. Say you want to make a big purchase, and you want to maximize the amount of time you have to save money to pay for it. Your billing cycle starts on March 26 and ends on April 25. Your payment due date is 21 days after the closing date, which means you need to make a payment on May 16. At what point during the billing period should you make your big purchase? If you buy it on April 24, the day before the end of the billing cycle, you'll still have to pay it back by May 16. This means you have just 22 days to pay it back. That's not too bad, but it might not be enough time. Now consider what happens if you make the purchase right at the beginning of the billing cycle, on March 26. The 21 days from the closing date to the payment due date is the same, but you get an extra 29 days, nearly an entire month before you have to pay. This should be more than enough time to raise the funds to pay the whole balance.

How can you use this to your greatest advantage? Ideally, you should try to make large purchases close to the beginning of the billing cycle as possible. This gives you almost two months to pay them off, and the whole time you'll know that you have to set aside enough money to cover the balance. With proper planning, you can bypass paying interest on the purchase entirely.

Of course, this method still means you must have enough money at the end of the two months to pay for the purchase in full. This isn't a magical money-printing machine or a way to get out of interest without being able to cover the cost of what you bought, but it can be an incredibly powerful tool that gives you enough time to deposit a few paychecks in your bank account before you need to pay off a purchase.

CAN YOU EXTEND THE GRACE PERIOD?

In most cases, you cannot extend your grace period, at least not permanently. It's possible to contact your card issuer and ask that your billing cycle be moved, which might give you an extra week or two. This is a good option if your payment date is just a few days before your payday, in which case you might have trouble covering your bills on time. Ask your lender if they can move your due date until after your payday to eliminate any conflicts. This can extend your grace period as an unintended side effect for one cycle, but it's far from a reliable solution. Starting the next month, you'll be back to the same grace period length since the whole billing cycle will shift. You may be able to use it to your advantage during a challenging month, but don't expect to get away with doing it multiple times.

Loan Grace Periods

Just like credit cards, loans can have grace periods too. You may not have to start making payments on a loan for anywhere between a few months to a few years after borrowing the money. While it's harder to extend your grace period for credit card debt, it's possible for student loans in certain situations. If you have a government subsidized loan, the loan won't accrue any interest until after you graduate. If you got the loan in your freshman year, you could skip four or more years of interest this way, though as soon as you graduate or drop out, interest will come back into play. In some cases, you can extend the grace period for both subsidized and unsubsidized loans, but usually only when specific conditions are met. If you return to school before the end of your regular grace period and you are at least a half-time student or if you're called to active military duty during this time, your lender may postpone mandatory loan payments until you are out of school or the military.

5

YOUR SCORE CARD

"The most important thing for a young man is to establish credit—a reputation and character."

— JOHN D. ROCKAFELLER

How good are you at borrowing and repaying money? This isn't exactly an easy question to answer, yet it's one that every lender must ask before agreeing to loan you any money. After all, they want to be sure that they'll make back the money they loaned you and ideally make a profit on it. They can't do that if you consistently miss payment deadlines or fail to pay back a loan entirely. Of course, a credit card company or a mortgage lender doesn't know much about you. They don't know your personality, your spending habits or how seriously you're going to take your responsibility to make payments on time. Additionally, they have to process requests from thousands to hundreds of thousands of people each day, depending on the company's size. How can they get a good idea of your trustworthiness as a borrower without taking the time to scrutinize every past debt of yours to determine if they should approve you for a new line of credit? The solution is your credit score.

Your credit score is like a report card for your borrowing habits. If you are a 'good' borrower who only borrows what you can afford to pay back and consistently keep up with minimum payments, companies are more willing to approve your application. If you're a 'bad' borrower who misses payments and expends more company resources when collections offices have to get involved, lenders may avoid doing business with you until you can improve your track record. Thankfully, you can always improve your credit score, no matter what it looks like right now. It may take some time for the positive changes you make to outweigh the previous negative ones, but in time you can bolster your credit and enjoy the optimal interest rates and other benefits that come with good credit.

Remember that your credit score doesn't necessarily reflect how much debt you have. You can have thousands of dollars of credit card debt and still have a great credit score because you only manage the minimum payments each month or you might consistently miss payments and drop your credit score while owing very little. While your credit score tells lenders how likely you are to pay them back on time, it doesn't tell them very much about your tendency to rack up debt. In fact, from the lender's perspective, it's better to loan money to someone who will only make minimum payments than it is to lend it to someone who pays the balance off in full every month; since in the former scenario, the lender makes more money on the interest accrued to your loan. Luckily, this can work out in your favor. You can improve your score even while you're still digging your way out of debt and you can do everything in your power to maintain a decent credit score even if you slip up and borrow too much money. As you learn more about how your credit score is calculated, you'll also understand how to avoid the mistakes that can cause lenders to see you as a 'bad' borrower and reject your credit applications.

BREAKING DOWN YOUR CREDIT SCORE

The vast majority of lenders evaluate your creditworthiness by looking at your FICO score. This is a three digit number that's calculated from your credit profile—namely, your available credit history. Your credit profile is reported by each of the three major credit bureaus: Experian, TransUnion, and Equifax. Typically, a lender will check just one of these when looking at your credit score.

FICO scores range from a minimum score of 300 to a maximum score of 850. This range is further divided into excellent, good, fair, and bad, so creditors can quickly determine whether your score is good or bad in general terms. The exact numeric cutoffs for each category can vary slightly, but typically, scores above 700 are considered good, with scores around 750 and above are seen as excellent. Scores between 650 to 700 are considered fair and any score below 650 is bad, usually reflecting an extensive history of mismanaged credit. The higher your score, the better interest rates, loan terms, and cardholder benefits you'll qualify for. With better rates and benefits, your debts will accrue less interest over time and you'll be in a better position to repay them before their interest rates get out of control.

Stay on top of your credit score, so you know how much work you will have to do to repair it. Turning a blind eye to a bad score doesn't make it go away. Instead, it makes it harder to avoid future repeats of past mistakes and leaves you in the dark about information that is readily available to creditors. Knowledge is power, after all, and knowing your credit score is the first step to repairing it.

Check Your Credit Score

Hold on a minute. Checking your credit score can hurt it, can't it? Sometimes, but not when you're checking your score. This is because of the difference between a hard pull and a soft pull.

A hard credit check, or pull, happens when a creditor makes an inquiry about your borrowing history. Hard inquiries can only occur with your expressed permission. For example, a lender may need to perform a hard inquiry before approving you for a personal loan or you might have your credit checked at a car dealership so you can be approved for a reasonable interest rate on your auto loan. Opening a new credit card or asking for a credit line increase both involve a hard inquiry. A lot of hard inquiries within a brief period of time can hurt your credit because it implies you may be opening more lines of credit than you can afford to pay off or that you open cards to reap the sign-on rewards and then cancel them. This may make creditors hesitant to lend you money, which is why you should try to limit hard inquiries to no more than three or four in a period of two years. However, the danger to your credit doesn't apply to the pre-approval notices you'll sometimes get in the mail. Since you didn't ask for them, they can't hurt your score. Rather than performing a hard pull, lenders only use a soft pull.

A soft inquiry is totally harmless to your credit score. When used by creditors, it's a way to get a general idea of your lending habits by skimming the surface of your credit history. They don't get the same extensive report they'd get with a hard inquiry, but they know enough to decide whether or not you'd be a good fit for their credit card or loan. While a pre-approval notice isn't a guarantee that you'll be approved, it's a pretty good sign. When you make a soft inquiry into your own credit, you can check your score for yourself in much the same way. You get a minimal amount of information, but you can check your score as often as you like and easily see how each missed or on-time payment impacts your score. You can use online tools to check your credit, but make sure you use a reputable site that's been around for a few years since you'll need to give personal information. Websites like Credit Karma and NerdWallet offer this feature for free.

Check Your Credit Report

While you can check your credit score as often as you'd like, checking your credit report is somewhat different. Your credit report provides a complete account of your borrowing history with plenty of specific, detailed information. You should check it occasionally to ensure there aren't any errors and know precisely what creditors see when they perform a hard credit inquiry. However, reviewing it too often can impact your credit and you may be required to pay a fee to do so.

Luckily, each of the three credit bureaus will provide you with your credit report once a year for free. You can obtain this by directly mailing a request form to the credit bureaus, but the easiest way is to use AnnualCreditReport.com, which will provide you with your full report from each of the three bureaus.

Now that you know what your credit score and credit report looks like, you can start improving them by tackling the factors that contribute most to low scores.

HOW YOUR CREDIT SCORE DROPS

If your credit score equates to your credit report card, then getting a bad grade in any 'subject' can bring down your total GPA. Some of these subjects are more obvious, such as the most significant reason—failing to make a payment on time. Other causes are less obvious, meaning you could be unknowingly harming your credit, even if you think you're improving it. Avoid these five missteps so you can efficiently repair your credit in as little time as possible.

Poor Payment History

Making timely payments is the best method for increasing your credit score, which of course, means that missing payment due dates are the best way to sink it. Your payment history accounts for about 35% of your credit score, making it the most significant factor. This means that just one missed payment can have an immediately noticeable effect on your credit. Even if your credit is otherwise amazing, a delinquent payment aged over a month past due can cause your current credit score to drop nearly 100 points. Let's say you've got a credit score of 710, which is in the 'good' range. Within a month, one missed payment could drop that score all the way down into the 'bad' range at 610, which might immediately disqualify you from better interest rates. If you already have a fair to poor credit score, you might end up being declined for new lines of credit, resulting in some difficulty when looking into refinancing options.

Of course, even knowing the importance of paying on time, it might still be hard to do so in practice. For one, unexpected financial emergencies happen, such as your car breaking down or losing your job. Paying the resulting bills generally takes precedence over credit card debt. You can easily avoid any uncertainty by giving yourself a buffer for emergency situations with your savings account. Save at least three months' worth of expenses as an emergency fund, though aiming for six or even twelve months is ideal. This way, if you find yourself without a reliable source of income or you need to pay an unexpected bill, you will avoid doing severe damage to your credit.

Additionally, poor planning can leave you with higher bills than you anticipated. As always, it's best to avoid buying more than you can afford to pay back whenever possible. Aside from cutting down on unnecessary spending, you can also try setting aside money in a separate bank account each time you make a purchase with your credit card. By the time you get your monthly bill, you should have enough in your account to pay it off in its entirety, which means you also get to take advantage of grace periods and interest-free lending. One word of caution; however, double check the minimum balance required to avoid monthly fees for your bank account. It's crucial never to drain the account altogether. Only withdraw what you need and keep the minimum balance in the account to avoid penalties or fees.

You may also have trouble remembering payment deadlines. To avoid this, set up automatic payments. Most cards allow you to set up a minimum monthly payment or pay the bill off in full. Just make sure you have enough money in your bank account, as this can result in overdraft fees if you're not paying attention.

Using up Too Much of Your Credit

Your available credit is a measure of all the credit you have under your name that you're not currently using. It's calculated by taking the sum of your credit lines and subtracting your total debts. For example, let's say you have two credit cards with credit limits of $3,200 and $1,300. You owe $1,250 on one and $1,000 on the other. This means you're using $2,250 of your available total of $4,500, or 50% of what's available to you. Even though you're still well below your upper limit on both cards, having too little available credit compared to your total credit limit can harm your score. It's usually best to pay down your debts, so you're using no more than 30% of your total credit limit at any given time, though less is always better.

Additionally, you want to avoid using up a lot of credit on any one card. Based on how your credit score is calculated, it's better to spread unpaid debts out on multiple cards than to wholly or nearly max out a card. Not only do maxed out cards hurt your credit, but they also rack up a lot of interest thanks to their high balances, so you should try to pay these off first.

If you're struggling to improve your credit, at least one person has probably suggested closing some of your credit cards. While this can help you curb your spending, this isn't always good for your credit, though it's a good idea for cards you don't often use that charge an annual cardholder fee. Even though you think you're saving your credit, you might be hurting it by lowering your available credit. You might feel like keeping around an old, infrequently used card is a waste, but a card with no debt on it can help balance out cards where you're using over 30% of your credit limit, so it might not be time to cancel it just yet. Still, it's possible a lender might cancel the card for you if it's unused for long enough, so consider making occasional small purchases on it and paying them off right away just to keep the card active.

One word of caution is that you should avoid opening new credit cards just for the sake of increasing your available credit. It's better to pay down existing debts to free up credit than it is to take on another line of credit and subconsciously encourage yourself to spend more with your shiny new card. Additionally, you run the risk of harming your credit by reducing your accounts' average age and increasing the number of recent credit checks on your report.

Brief Credit Age

The more extensive your credit history is, the easier it is for lenders to get a good picture of your borrowing habits. If most of your credit accounts are brand new, you haven't had time to prove to lenders that you're trustworthy. Credit age only accounts for about 15% of your FICO score, so it's far from the single most important factor, but it's still something to consider before closing older accounts or opening newer ones.

A very short credit history can also amplify the effects of delinquency. If you only have a few years' worth of payment history and you've been delinquent on at least one account for multiple months during that time, it's going to look worse than if you've had cards that have remained in good standing for a decade or longer. With a more extensive credit history, the mistakes are balanced out by your otherwise proven reliability. When there's only a limited sample of data for a lender to base their decision on, missed payments are a much bigger deal, and they have more power to harm your score.

Recent Credit Checks

Soft credit checks might not affect your credit, but hard checks do. Each time a lender checks your credit, whether you're trying to get approved for a new loan or you want to renegotiate the terms of an existing line of credit, their hard check remains on your report for as long as two years. You should try to keep the number of visible credit checks under about two or three to keep your credit score high. While this might sound simple, it's a little more complicated in practice since these credit checks can add up if you request multiple hard pulls within a short time frame. If you need an auto loan, a student loan, and a new credit card all in the same year, you're already pushing the limit, and these checks stay on your report whether or not your application is approved.

Try to space out hard checks as much as possible to keep them from hurting your score. They only account for about 10% of how your score is calculated, but this 10% could mean the difference between having your credit labeled as fair or poor in some cases. You can minimize the impact this has on your score by spacing out applications for new lines of credit and prioritizing things you've been preapproved for, minimizing your need to shop around at different companies.

No Credit Account Type Diversity

Lenders like to see that you have a decent diversity of different credit sources on your report. They might look more favorably upon your application if you have a student loan, a mortgage, and a credit card than if you simply have three credit cards. If they know you can successfully manage different credit types, they'll be more likely to approve you for future loans. If you want to know if your credit mix is good enough, you'll first need to know the difference between installment and revolving credit.

Most loans count as a type of installment credit. You have a fixed loan length and even payments each month as you pay back the balance. Unless the terms of the loan change or you decide to pay more to repay the loan faster, the amount you set aside for installment payments shouldn't change. Different types of installment loans include student loans, mortgages, personal loans, and auto loans.

Revolving credit on the other hand, includes less consistent monthly payments like those you would see with credit cards, whether they're issued by a retail store or a bank. The amount you owe each billing period is determined by how much you spent during it. You have more control over the debt burden you take on at any time, but you can also quickly get yourself into trouble by spending too much. To have a good credit mix, you'll need both installment and revolving credit types on your credit report. This means the accounts must be open and active to count.

Like hard credit checks, a lack of credit diversity is a minimal factor, but it's still one to consider when trying to build, rebuild, or maintain your credit score. Still, avoid taking out a new loan if you don't actually need one. Try to avoid having too many accounts open that fall into either category.

SCORE ACCURACY BETWEEN BUREAUS

Sometimes your credit score will be a few points different depending on what credit bureau is reporting it. Does this mean there was fraud on your account or some other error? Sometimes, but it's not likely and there's no need to panic right away. It's perfectly normal for your score to vary between different credit bureaus because certain institutions might report credit information to just one or two of the three bureaus.

When I worked at a credit union, we only reported information to Experian and Equifax and didn't submit borrower information to TransUnion. Borrowers who were customers of our credit union would have seen the effects of their payments —or lack thereof—on two of their credit scores, but not on the TransUnion one. This is a cost-saving measure on the lender's part and typically it won't affect your credit score in a significant way. As long as you check your credit report from each bureau once a year and report any inaccuracies, you can be confident your scores are error-free, even if they're off by a few points.

Your FICO score is compiled based on information provided by all three major credit bureaus, and it's generally regarded as the most accurate measure of your credit health. Many sites with access to your credit information, such as different credit card companies, can also provide you with your FICO score.

HOW DEBT AFFECTS CREDIT

Debt can negatively impact your credit in many different ways. For one, as you get deeper into debt, you'll have more trouble repaying those debts. Interest builds up each month and it becomes more difficult to make even minimum payments on time. Additionally, too much debt can wipe out your available credit, as previously mentioned. The higher the balance is on each of your cards, the less available credit you'll have, and the worse this will reflect on your credit score. This isn't just a concern for credit cards; failure to pay off high loan balances can hurt your score, too.

The faster you can repay your debts, the lower your credit utilization ratio will be, keeping your credit score high. Failing to pay back what you owe because your debt to income ratio is too high is a major red flag to new lenders since this means you probably won't be able to pay them back either. How you decide to handle your debt once you can no longer keep up with payments can hurt your score too. Whether you settle your debts, consolidate them, or declare bankruptcy, your credit score takes a hit, though bankruptcy has the most long-lasting effect on your credit. Either way, being unable to appropriately manage your debt has severe repercussions for your credit that you don't want to face if you can help it. One of the best preventative measures you can take is considering your debt-to-income ratio before doing any borrowing.

Your Debt-to-Income Ratio

Unlike many of the other topics we've discussed in this chapter, your debt-to-income (DTI) ratio isn't directly involved in calculating your credit score. However, it can still be a factor when getting approved for a loan or other line of credit and a poor debt-to-income ratio is a recipe for disaster for any borrower.

As the name implies, this ratio represents the difference between your earnings and your debts. It includes all sources of income, such as your paycheck and your investment revenue, as well as all types of debts you hold. This means debts from both revolving and installment credit lines as well as any other routine monthly payments like rent or alimony. To calculate your DTI, simply add up your average monthly debt and divide it by your monthly income. Multiply this number by 100 to convert it to a percentage. You want your DTI ratio to be as small as possible. Around 35% or less is a good goal for most people. If you have 50% or more of your monthly income tied up in paying off debts, you should strongly avoid taking on additional debt before paying down what you owe. Of course, you can also improve your DTI ratio by increasing your income, but this is often out of your immediate control, so I'll focus on paying off debts for now.

You can lower your DTI ratio over time by making more than the minimum required payment on your credit card debt and loans. You don't need to pay thousands of dollars all at once to make a significant dent in what you owe; just increasing your payments by $50 or $100 over the minimum can really add up over time. This is one of the most reliable ways to pay down large amounts of debt without straining your bank account too much.

In some cases, you may need to consider more significant lifestyle changes that free up more of your income, such as downsizing your home or trading in your more modern car for one with a few more years under its fan belt. This is a valuable move if you've been living well outside your means and you need to make a serious change to cut back on your expenses. You don't want to escape debt just to fall right back into it, after all, and this goes double for restoring your credit score.

BUILDING CREDIT

As you improve your DTI ratio and start to chip away at the mounds of debt that have been plaguing you for months or years, you'll also start rebuilding your credit. We often think of building credit as a slow and arduous process, but it doesn't have to take years to make improvements. You can raise lousy credit to fair or good levels relatively quickly just by making a few small changes, which may be the jumpstart you need to restore your credit score. In addition to sticking to the advice I've previously discussed, like making payments on time and disputing errors, you can also turn your credit around by raising your credit limits, making payments more often, switching to a secured credit card, or becoming an authorized user on someone else's account.

Ask for a Higher Credit Limit

Having more available credit can improve your score, but that doesn't mean you should go rushing off to open many new cards. Instead, you might consider increasing the credit limits on your current cards. If you stop spending on these cards altogether, this will immediately improve your score. Keep in mind that sometimes this still requires the lender to perform a hard credit check, but you can often get an increase in your credit limit without one, especially if you've been making an effort to make payments on time recently. In fact, if you consistently pay your balance in full for multiple months in a row, your lender may automatically raise your credit limit without the need for a request. You may also have an easier time securing an increase if your income recently increased.

Pay Bimonthly or Weekly

If you make payments on your loans or credit card debt just once each month, consider making two or three micropayments instead. You'll end up paying the same amount, but your credit utilization will decrease faster since you're paying off half or a third of your monthly bill at the beginning of the billing period rather than at the end. Additionally, anything you're able to pay off won't continue accruing interest, which will lower your total debt.

Use a Secured Credit Card

Most credit cards are unsecured, which means you can spend as much as you like each month up to your credit limit and then pay this back over time. While unsecured cards usually have better rates and benefits, they also encourage high spending. With a secured card, you put down a cash deposit at the beginning of the billing period, which becomes a hard limit for how much you can spend each month. This means you'll always have enough money to pay the card off, so you can consistently make on-time full payments and build your credit very quickly. Once you've repaired your credit and turned these better borrowing practices into lifelong habits, you can usually convert a secured card into an unsecured one and continue using it without having to close the account or apply with a different lender.

Take Advantage of Being an Authorized User

Do you know someone in your life who has an excellent credit history and who might be willing to help you rebuild your own? Consider becoming an authorized user on one of their credit card accounts. As an authorized user, you can practice borrowing and repaying with less risk to your own credit, with the assistance of your friend or family member. If you both practice good borrowing habits, both of your credit scores will increase. Of course, you don't actually have to use the card to reap the benefits for your credit score. Just having your name on the account while the account holder makes purchases and pays them back can boost your score by default.

There are many ways to repair a poor credit score. With smart borrowing habits, you can raise a bad or mediocre score all the way up to good or even excellent credit; it's never too late to improve your score, just like it's never too late to eliminate your debt.

6

CENTRALIZE YOUR DEBT

"As long as a person is breathing, there is hope for them."

— ANTHONY KIEDIS

C redit lines, loans, and other sources of debt build up naturally over time. You might have five or more different credit cards that you opened over a ten year period. Maybe you financed each year of college through another loan servicer. There may be various medical bills from different appointments and multiple offices you're still paying off months or years later. While it's perfectly normal to have debt from various sources, this can make paying those debts off a little more complex.

When you have many different debt sources, it's easy to lose track of how much you owe on which accounts and the total amount you should be setting aside each month to make payments. Additionally, even minimum payments can really add up when you have ten or more accounts, each asking you for $200 or $300 each month. This can quickly overwhelm you and make you more likely to miss payments entirely. It is an even bigger problem when you consider that most credit cards have relatively high interest rates, which means every month you go without paying off your debt in full will cost you severely.

Enter debt consolidation. When you consolidate your debts, a single lender takes over multiple existing debts, often with lower interest rates and an adjusted repayment schedule. Rather than sending money to dozens of lenders and losing track of where it needs to go, you only have to make one payment each month, so it's easier to save exactly as much as you need. Your minimum monthly payment is typically lower too since you don't have to pay multiple creditors. When used smartly and only when necessary, centralizing your debt with a single lender can simplify the repayment process and help you repay your debts at a fraction of the time and cost of your current contracts.

HOW HELPFUL IS CONSOLIDATING?

Debt consolidation likely sounds like a dream come true, and in many cases, it can be an excellent strategy. It may give you the jumpstart you need to escape endless repayment and become debt-free in as little as five years, depending on how much you can afford to pay at once. That said, it's important to weigh the pros and cons of consolidation before you leap into it. There are some cases where it can make things more difficult for you by exacerbating bad financial habits. Consider all the benefits and consequences that come with centralizing your debt before you commit to consolidation, as this isn't a process you can undo.

The Benefits of Consolidating

Debt consolidation can be highly beneficial if you're having trouble paying off extensive credit card debt and high-interest loans. Let's say you have multiple credit cards with outstanding balances, and these cards all have APRs of 20-30%. In this case, you'd end up spending a lot of money trying to pay these cards off over time. Each time you made a payment, the high APRs would significantly increase what you owed, making your payments much less effective than they would be otherwise. Consolidation, in this scenario, would be a great idea. You might also qualify for a low-interest, fixed rate personal loan that could help you quickly pay off this debt in a few years without significant hassle. If you can afford to make payments above the monthly minimum, you'll pay it off much faster, but even if you need more time, the 2-5% interest rate you might qualify for is leagues better than what you were previously dealing with.

Consolidating is sometimes a good idea, even if you don't have a large amount of debt. If you qualify for a balance-transfer credit card, many of which offer 0% interest for a year or longer, you can cut through your debts without them accruing any more interest. Of course, to take full advantage of the 0% interest, you'll need to be able to pay off what you owe during that initial period. The debt changes hands and you don't have to worry about interest accrual for a few months, but this doesn't eliminate any of your current obligations; it's up to you to pay your debt off. Additionally, it's still a credit card with a credit limit, so chances are you won't be able to put something like a student loan on it. Balance-transfer cards are great when you owe a few thousand dollars, but if your debts are higher than that, it might be a better idea to consolidate with a loan instead. Consolidation loans typically have lower credit requirements for approval than balance-transfer cards, too, though you might not get the best rates if you have poor credit.

Consolidation Pitfalls

Unfortunately, for all of consolidation's benefits, not everything is sunshine and roses. For starters, the usefulness of your loan or balance-transfer card is mainly dependent on your credit score. The whole point of consolidating is getting a lower interest rate, but if your credit has gotten worse in recent years due to missed payments, you might only be approved for a rate that's the same or worse than what you had before. If this is the case, it's probably a good idea to avoid consolidation until you've improved your score.

Additionally, what initially seems like an enticing interest rate may increase over time. Balance-transfer cards might have 0% interest rates at first, but a few months down the line, the interest rate may increase to more than what was on your previous cards when this initial period ends. If you can pay off your debt within that initial period, that's great, but if you can't, you might end up in more debt than before.

Another angle to consider is that while consolidation can ostensibly help you pay off what you owe quickly, they often result in you remaining in debt for much longer. Your interest rate goes down, but to make up for it, the loan term is extended for the trade-off of lowering your monthly payment. When lenders extend the term of the loan, not only will it take you longer to become debt-free, but you also end up paying a decent amount of interest. This can, and often does, amount to higher total payments than what you would have paid without consolidating; after all, lenders want to make money off of you and interest is the best way to do so. You can avoid this by making more than the minimum payments and getting ahead of schedule, but if you don't think you can hold yourself to this, consolidation may not be the best option for you.

Finally, consolidation itself does nothing to prevent you from getting into debt again. It is a valuable tool, but if you keep spending like you did when you racked up all that debt in the first place, you're only going to continue repeating the process over and over. Therefore, any effective use of debt consolidation must also be combined with a plan for staying out of debt in the future.

Consolidation and Your Debt-Free Plan

Consolidation is not a magical cure-all for debt troubles. It won't reduce the balance you owe and as you've just read, it can sometimes make your debt issues even worse if you don't carefully check the details of the plan or if you become more complacent about paying back what you owe. That said, it has plenty of benefits too. In many cases, you can get a much lower interest rate and it's often easier to keep track of a single payment rather than trying to manage a dozen different credit card bills. You can't treat consolidation like a debt panacea, but it can give you a notable advantage in many cases.

Before consolidating any credit card or loan debt, consider if the consolidation loan terms are better or worse than what you're already dealing with. For example, if you have a student loan from a federal loan servicer, you might qualify for income-driven repayment, which will shrink your monthly payments to

CENTRALIZE YOUR DEBT | 91

fit only what your current income can afford. In some cases, you may not have a monthly minimum at all, though you should still try to pay a little off to keep interest down. Consolidating a loan where you owe nothing or very little is typically the wrong move since the same income-driven repayment plan would no longer be available to you. The same is true for any debt where the current interest rate is lower than that of the consolidation loan. Ensure you're giving yourself an advantage when you consolidate, and you're not missing out on great benefits. Remember that you don't have to cram every single debt you have under one loan so that you may be better off only consolidating a select few with high interest rates like credit card debt. If consolidation really is a better offer, then it can be a great opportunity, but make sure it's a good choice for your situation first.

Rather than relying entirely on consolidation or completely ignoring it as an option, make this a piece of your debt relief puzzle. Use it alongside other strategies like paying more than the minimum balance and splitting your payments up, so they're bi-monthly or even weekly. This way, you're reducing your interest rates and paying your loans off quicker, which means you really will end up paying less to get out of debt. Additionally, raising your credit score can make consolidation a more attractive option. Furthermore, a better credit score is more likely to help you qualify for the best interest rates and loan terms. When combined with a clear plan for debt repayment, you can get more mileage out of your credit and put a more significant dent in what you owe, allowing you to get out of debt much faster.

WHICH DEBT TO PAY OFF FIRST

Consolidation is so attractive because it decreases the interest rate on the balances you owe. As you might imagine, it makes sense to pay off your high-interest debts first and foremost. These debts will increase in value exponentially faster than balances with a low interest rate, so letting them linger for too long is more damaging. This is known as the "debt avalanche" method, and it's generally seen as the method that will help you save the most money. However, certain considerations to make when using this method, especially when combined with consolidation, will determine just how effective it is for you. Additionally, it's far from the only way to put a dent in what you owe. While it has its given drawbacks, you might consider the "debt snowball" method instead, which involves paying off smaller debts first and working your way up to more challenging ones. The process you should choose depends on your situation and what motivates you to make payments.

THE DEBT AVALANCHE

The debt avalanche method involves looking at each of your sources of debt, listing them in order from the highest APR to the lowest, and then paying off each one in turn. When you start with the highest APR debts first, you prevent them from accruing more interest, continually paying down your balance and reducing the amount of interest you owe each month until you are entirely debt-free on one account. Then you can move on to paying off the debt with the next highest interest rate and tackle each one in order of urgency. Typically, credit cards are first in a debt avalanche since they tend to have the highest interest rates compared to loans, medical debt, and debts to the government.

The debt avalanche's central goal is to spend as little total money as possible while making payments. However, in some cases, following conventional advice doesn't actually help you achieve this goal. In fact, there are some cases where it might be wiser to pay off a lower interest debt first rather than following the avalanche method. Common points of contention include the size of the balance you owe, whether a debt is secured or unsecured, and whether or not you decide to consolidate.

Calculating Interest

The general consensus is that a higher interest rate means you'll owe more in interest than debts with lower interest rates. This is usually true, but it might not be if the starting balances are significantly different. Remember that interest is a fraction of what you already owe. If you have a line of credit with a very high interest rate, but the debt itself is minimal, the interest accrued each month might still be less than a reasonably low interest rate where the balance on your loan is very high.

Consider the following example: let's say you have a $500 debt on one of your credit cards, with an APR of 30%, which is relatively high. You also have a $3,000 debt on another card with a fairly low APR of 12%. After a year, you'd owe an additional $150 on the first debt. As for the second, you'd have to pay an additional $360. Even though the first debt had an interest rate that was more than double the second, it still accrued less than half as much interest because the balance on the account was much lower. Therefore, you would save more money if you paid off the second debt before the first. This is why going off APR alone might not help you identify the most expensive debts. Go to https://allenanything.com to obtain my Debt Decimator and Budgeting Workbook to determine which debt to pay off first.

Consolidation and the Debt Avalanche

Normally, you would begin a debt avalanche by making a payment on the debt with the highest interest, but what happens if you choose to consolidate your debts instead? Consolidation typically lowers the rate on your loans, which means what was previously your most urgent debt might become your lowest priority.

Of course, consolidation should never mean a debt falls entirely off your radar. It might push the debt a little further down your priority list, but you should still keep making at least the minimum payments and you should still try to pay the debt off sooner rather than later. Keep in mind that consolidation might have a lower interest rate. Still, as previously mentioned, it may have a higher balance, therefore, more accrued interest, mainly since it includes the balances from multiple debts. Consider how much more expensive the interest on a consolidated loan will be, compared to high-interest, low-balance debts before deciding where to place it on your priority list.

Secured Versus Unsecured Debts

Another situation in which you might choose to prioritize a debt with a lower interest rate is if that debt is secured. If a debt, typically a loan, is secured, it means you've put up collateral that the lender can take if you fail to make payments on time. Essentially, you're making a bet that you won't fall behind on payments. With a mortgage, you put up your home as collateral. With an auto loan, your collateral is your car.

As you might imagine, falling behind on a secured loan can have significant consequences. If you continually miss mortgage or auto loan payments, you might find your home in foreclosure or your car repossessed. This scenario can be devastating, so it's best to prioritize your secured loans.

Even if you follow the debt avalanche method, it's important to prioritize making at least the minimum payments on secured loans. You don't necessarily have to pay them off first, no one would suggest you completely pay off your mortgage before making any payments on your credit card debt, but you need to pay the bare minimum to avoid repossession and foreclosure.

Set aside the money you need for your secured loans first, then pool the rest of your resources into your high-interest unsecured debts.

THE DEBT SNOWBALL

Another standard method for becoming debt-free is the debt snowball method. In this method, you ignore the APRs of your debts and instead try to pay off your smallest debt first. This should be very easy. Paying off your small debts might not save you a lot in interest, but it might motivate you more effectively than the debt avalanche, where you might have to wait months before you can say you've completely paid off any debt. Each successful closure of small debt becomes momentum you use to tackle larger loans, eventually working your way up to your most enormous debts.

This method is generally more expensive than the avalanche method since high-interest debts might go unpaid for a while and you'll be racking up a lot of interest on your bigger loans until you finally get to them. Still, it has its uses, especially if you've tried more conventional repayment plans in the past and have had trouble sticking to them. The little burst of motivation with each payoff might be exactly what you need to stick to your debt-free plan.

While the snowball method can be a great motivational tool, it usually doesn't pair well with debt consolidation. When you consolidate your debts, you make them much larger, which would push them further down the list. Whether the interest rate is high or low, these large sums of debt will accrue a lot of interest by the time you get to them. If you want to use the debt snowball method, consolidating your debts may not be the best move, as you can end up in a lot more debt if you're not careful.

CONSOLIDATION VERSUS REFINANCING

Aside from debt consolidation, you also have the option of refinancing. While both consolidation and refinancing involves taking your current debt and altering the initial terms, they operate very differently and you shouldn't use them interchangeably. When you refinance, you don't combine your debts into one. Instead, you look at each loan individually, identifying which ones might have better terms available to you now than when you first got them. You then change the terms just for these loans, typically by applying for a new loan and using that to pay off the old one.

Refinancing is usually a good choice if either the market or your specific circumstances have changed significantly since you initially took out your loan. For example, maybe the housing market was different when you moved into your current home and mortgage rates were higher, but they've since fallen. This doesn't help you get a better rate on your credit card, but it might help you get a better home loan if you refinance. You can take out a new mortgage at the improved rate, pay off the old mortgage in full, then pay the new mortgage the same way you would any other loan. Ideally, you'll get either a better interest rate, a shorter loan period, or cheaper monthly payments. You may even use refinancing to secure a different loan type altogether, like turning a variable rate loan into one with a fixed rate.

Fixed rate loans maintain the same interest rate for the life of the loan. They aren't affected by changes in the market which might otherwise increase interest rates across the board. A variable rate, on the other hand, can change according to market conditions. Variable loans usually start with lower interest rates than fixed ones, which may sound more attractive at first, but inflation and rising costs means the rate increases significantly over time. While there's a chance your rate may decrease, more often than not, the longer you take to pay back your variable loan, the higher your interest rate will be. If you can pay the loan off quickly while it's still at a reasonably low interest rate, a variable loan could work for you, but fixed rates are typically a better idea if you know you'll take the whole loan term to pay it off.

Just like consolidation, refinancing may be suitable for some people and not for others. If you want to restructure your debts, start by deciding whether you should consolidate or refinance.

Deciding Which Option Is Best for You

Both consolidation and refinancing are good options in different circumstances. As previously mentioned, refinancing is an attractive option when something has changed and there are better rates available to you. This might mean the loan market itself or it might mean your credit score has improved and you're qualified for better loans. Of course, an improvement to your credit score might qualify you for very low interest rates when you consolidate too, which can help you manage much more of your debts at once.

Another vital factor to consider is how much difficulty you have keeping up with a larger number of payments. Are you financially well-off enough to set up automatic payments for the recurring charges? Do you have to pay each one individually and adjust according to how much you can afford each month? In the latter case, consolidation is probably the better option since you'll only have one lower monthly payment to worry about for many sources of debt. If you have no trouble keeping track of multiple payments and you'd like to avoid having any one of them become too large, then refinancing is a more suitable option. It may also be the better option if you're only having difficulty with particular debts, as you can focus on getting better rates for these without rolling in additional debts that aren't an issue for you.

Ultimately, whether you choose to consolidate, refinance, or do neither is up to you and your current circumstances. Additionally, you may be able to refinance and consolidate depending on your lenders' terms and conditions and whether this is beneficial for your situation. There is no one option that is inherently better than the others. It is your responsibility to evaluate how sound each strategy would be for your individual situation to finally become debt-free.

7

NEGOTIATING WITH CREDITORS

> *"Let us never negotiate out of fear. But let us never fear to negotiate."*
>
> — JOHN F. KENNEDY

Many people have the mindset that when you owe a debt, creditors are your enemy. They want to steal all of your money and offer you nothing in return and they'll drive you to bankruptcy to do it. They don't want to hear any of your excuses about why you can't afford your current minimum payments and talking to your lenders won't do you any favors, so why bother? This is a popular line of thinking, but it is not actually true.

While some creditors operate this way, the vast majority of them are willing to work with you to create a repayment plan that works for everyone. Think of things from their perspective. They make money through interest, yes, but they don't make any money at all if you fail to pay them back. They'll lose a big portion of what they've lent to you if they need to send your bill to collections. They'll lose even more if you're forced to declare bankruptcy and they end up writing off the loaned money entirely. Looking at the issue this way, if your lender was given a choice between receiving all the money you owe them later, receiving only a tiny fraction of it right away, or getting none at all, they would almost certainly choose the first option. Suppose you can't afford to repay your loan with its current terms. In that case, it's worth asking your creditor if they'd be willing to adjust the terms and assist you in coming up with a new payment plan, even if repayment ends up taking longer than anticipated.

Ultimately, the worst thing you can do is ignore your creditor when trying to collect on your debt and hope it simply disappears. As we covered in Chapter Three, delinquent debt doesn't vanish and a collections agency might be much less willing to negotiate with you than your lender. If you're proactive about bringing a problem to your creditor's attention, they can help you sort it out.

Still, negotiations aren't always as straightforward as admitting you need help. While lenders aren't necessarily your sworn enemies, they aren't your friends either. If you go into negotiations unprepared, you might not get the best rate available, all because you aren't sure how to "play the game." Learn the best ways to bargain with lenders to ensure you're getting access to the best possible options for your credit score and amount of debt.

STRATEGIES FOR NEGOTIATING INTEREST RATE

When negotiating, keep in mind that the interest rate you were given when you first got your credit card or loan isn't permanent. Your lender might want you to think it is, but it's actually a pretty flexible number. Check online to see if they offer lower interest rates than the one on your card currently. You might not get the lowest rate, but it's likely you can bring your current interest rate down quite a bit and it helps to know what your baseline is.

You can typically request a reduction just by picking up the phone and giving your creditor a call, but you'll want to consider your strategy before you begin.

Have All Information Readily Accessible

When you call to negotiate, your lender will ask you for relevant information like your current balance and APR, the statement due date, and other card details such as your account number and the card's grace period. You should also have your salary information and a safe estimate of how much you can afford to pay each month, which will help you determine how low an interest rate you're shooting for. You don't want to be scrambling for this information and have to ask the representative from your lender to hold while you look for it, so keep everything with you when you call and make sure you can quickly look up any information you need. Consider writing relevant details down ahead of time, especially if you need to research something, such as how low of an APR your lender currently offers.

Staying organized has the added benefit of making you come off as knowledgeable and confident, which will do a lot more to persuade your lender than if you seem uncertain. Remember that you're negotiating, not asking for a favor from a friend, which means you have to sound like you won't take no for an answer.

Pit Lenders Against Each Other

In most cases, your current lender wants to keep your business. However, if you can get a better deal somewhere else, there's no reason for you not to jump ship. Even if you don't plan on switching, pitting lenders against each other is a great way to make sure you're getting the best possible rate from your current lender.

Start by selecting a card your credit score would likely qualify you for. See if they're willing to do a soft credit check and tell you what you can expect for your card's APR. If it isn't lower than what you're already paying, keep looking. Once you have a competitive offer, call or email your current lender and say you're considering closing your account in favor of opening one with another lender. Then ask if they can match or do better than the other lender's APR. If they can, repeat this process with the first lender. Eventually, both companies will reach a point where they can't go any lower, but this is probably quite a bit lower than the APR you originally qualified for. You've effectively reduced your APR and you didn't have to improve your credit or pay off a huge chunk of your balance, though these should be your next steps if you want to take advantage of your new interest rate.

You can repeat this process to reduce the APR of loans, too. If you haven't taken out a loan yet, ask companies about price matching before moving forward. Tell them you're genuinely interested in taking out a loan with them, but you don't want to pass up on a great deal with the other lender. If you already have a loan, you can look into refinancing and consolidation to find competitive APRs. Most lenders will quote you an APR with a soft credit check in minutes on their websites, so there's no harm in checking as many different companies as possible before committing to one.

Try Asking for a Temporary Reduction

Your lender might not be willing to reduce your APR permanently, but they may be willing to do it for a few months.

Let them know that you're struggling to pay all your bills right now and that you just need a lower rate until you can pay off your debts and get back on your feet. It also helps to explain how you're planning on improving your financial situation in the future. For example, maybe you're looking for a new job or you're starting to budget your money so you can always pay off future credit card bills. This shows them you're taking the initiative to get yourself out of debt rather than being solely reliant on their assistance. You want to pay off your debt, but you just can't manage it at the current interest rate. If your lender lowers your APR, even for just a few months, this can make a huge difference in how quickly you're able to become debt-free.

Don't Be Afraid to Switch Lenders

Unfortunately, not every negotiation will end in success. Sometimes your lender will simply refuse to negotiate your rate any lower with you. However, other lenders might be offering better rates, which you should take advantage of. If you can't negotiate further and there are better options available, there's no reason not to switch lenders. In some cases, when you move to close your card, you'll be offered a better rate to convince you to stay. If not, you can leave guilt-free and move on to a better lender.

Keep in mind that closing an account doesn't mean all your credit card debt miraculously goes away. You'll either have to transfer the balance to your new credit card or continue to pay it off slowly over time, as you've been doing.

HOW TO IMPROVE YOUR CHANCES

Even if you have the best negotiation skills in the world, you might still have some trouble finding a lower rate if you have a poor credit score or a spotty payment history. To ensure you have the best chances of getting approved for a lower APR, whether you're looking for a new card or trying to adjust the terms of your current one, you can improve your chances by making on-time payments routinely, having a cosigner, and scouting out great deals.

Have a Good Track Record

It should come as no surprise that if you're frequently delinquent on your payments, your lender probably isn't going to look favorably upon your request for a lower interest rate. You want to come off as someone who is reliable and prepared to pay back anything you borrow, even if you've been having trouble lately due to high interest rates. If you need an interest rate adjustment, you probably can't afford to pay off the entire balance of your card right now, but you should still be able to make the minimum payments on time for a few months. If lenders see you can stick to the repayment schedule, they're more likely to offer you a better interest rate, even if your credit isn't ideal.

Get a Cosigner

Maybe you have poor credit, but a reliable friend or family member has excellent credit. In this case, you can ask them to be a cosigner on your loan. A cosigner with stellar credit can help you qualify for better interest rates, as your lender can be more confident that you or your cosigner will pay them back. Cosigners can also balance out a high amount of existing debt or a low-paying job if they're in a better financial situation. Additionally, making on-time payments means both you and your cosigner get a boost to your credit.

However, before asking anyone to be your cosigner, make sure they know the risks they're taking on. Having multiple names listed on a loan is a little like doing a group project together. If you succeed at making payments on time, you succeed together. If you fail, you fail together. The lender will turn to your cosigner if they find you've been unable to pay back your loan. They may even be at risk of being sued if you fall behind on monthly payments. Therefore, only choose someone you know well and consider how a missed payment would not only impact your friend or family member, but also how it might strain your relationship. If you're worried money matters might come between you, it might be best to stick to loans you qualify for on your own.

Look for Promotional Offers

Many credit card companies offer starting rates that are significantly lower than their usual rates. In some cases, you can even enjoy a 0% APR for anywhere from a few months to two years after you open your card as long as you keep up with minimum payments. Most cards that offer this are known as balance-transfer cards and they're an excellent option if you're looking to switch lenders. Use them to pay for all the debts you owe on your previous card, transferring the balance to the new one. Then you have a few months to pay back this balance interest-free on your new card.

One thing to keep in mind, however, is that intro APRs only last so long. Once this initial period is over, you'll have to start paying interest again. Worse, in many cases, your lender might apply all the interest you otherwise would have accrued during that time to your current balance. This is why it's imperative to take full advantage of a 0% intro APR and pay off all debts on the card during this window. Don't let the lack of interest make you complacent or it'll come back to haunt you later.

Some cards may have additional promotional offers, such as a rewards program. You may be able to get great cashback rates, which means a small percentage of what you spend on all qualifying purchases is refunded to you. You can then apply this balance to your monthly payments, reducing the amount you owe. Alternatively, credit card companies may offer rewards in the form of 'points,' which can then be used for discounts at various stores, exchanged for gift cards, or turned into airline miles. Consider which type of reward would save you the most money with your everyday lifestyle when choosing a new credit card. If you fly often, you might get the most incredible benefits out of a card that offers airline miles, but if you rarely fly, you might be better off with a card that helps you save on everyday purchases like gas and groceries. The terms for each card are different, so consider them carefully before completing an application. The right card can help you save a lot of money.

8

SAVING CHANGE TO CHANGE THE WAY YOU SAVE

"I don't look to jump over seven-foot bars: I look around for one-foot bars that I can step over."

— WARREN BUFFET

W e've talked a lot about your habits as a borrower so far, but what about your spending habits? After all, the best way to avoid debt is to avoid overspending. You won't have to spend time and money paying back months' worth of interest if you can curb your spending habits, so debt never has the chance to pile up. Still, this may be easier said than done, particularly if you've struggled with debt for many years. You may have gotten yourself into a destructive pattern of making too many purchases, spending too much money, and going even deeper into debt trying to dig yourself out of it. You might even go on a shopping spree to manage your stress, which only makes your situation worse. You don't have to make big purchases for your debt to spiral out of control and wreck your wallet and your credit.

As is the case with all habits, small actions can multiply and have enormous consequences. Let's say you typically buy lunch on the days you work. With a standard nine-to-five full-time job, this means you're buying your lunch five days a week. Your lunch costs an average of $12, and you pay for it with your credit card. After a week, you've spent $60. After a month, you're already up to $240. Lunch itself isn't expensive, but these small purchases add up over time. If you don't pay your credit card off in full, that means you're paying interest on the remainder you haven't paid off. Keep buying lunch every week and failing to pay it off and you'll end up with a huge bill just from a few sandwiches. Even if you don't put these payments on your credit card, they can eat into the money in your bank account that you could otherwise put toward making debt payments. Now let's say you decide to make lunch at home, so you spend about $20 for a weeks' worth of sandwich supplies. You've already reduced how much you're spending by two-thirds with this one change, leaving you with more money for paying down debt and better credit. You didn't make a huge change, but the positive effects continued adding up over time, becoming much greater than the sum of their parts.

Following good spending and saving habits is just as important as cutting back on bad ones. For spending, this can be as simple as waiting five minutes before you make any kind of purchase. This gives you time to consider whether you really need it or not and take yourself out of the *I have to buy this right now* mindset that can cause you to buy things that only end up collecting dust at the back of your closet. If you need something a little more concrete, you can try writing out a budget for yourself and using that to decide what you can and can't afford to buy, even if you use credit. As for saving habits, it's good to practice saving a small portion of each paycheck, so you're always making a contribution. Just $100 every two weeks adds up to $2,600 a year. Without significantly cutting back, you can build up a comfortable cushion of savings as an emergency fund or pay this toward your debts until you're completely debt-free. If you have the option, you may be able to split your direct deposit, so a portion goes directly into your savings account, making the process automatic. The more you save, the more prepared you'll be for future financial emergencies and the less debt you'll end up in when they happen.

Remember that there is a psychological component to spending, especially if you feel like your spending habits are almost compulsory. Changing your spending habits might not be as easy as telling yourself to spend less. For example, stressful events and bad moods may drive you to seek out the instant gratification of making a purchase. Spending feels good in the moment, but it's only later that you might start regretting exchanging your savings for such a brief spike of happiness, especially if this only worsens your debt trouble. This can then become a vicious cycle, where financial stress sends you looking for a quick pick-me-up once again.

Breaking this cycle means letting go of the need for instant gratification and learning to accept that getting out of debt will require some hard work and discomfort. You'll have to get comfortable with telling yourself *no*, or at least *not yet*. You'll also need to keep an eye out for the events and feelings that trigger your spending habits, like complex projects at work or a lack of sleep and replace spending with healthier habits that address the root cause of these issues. Repeated excessive spending isn't an isolated incident; consider how other aspects of your life are subtly encouraging you to look for relief in making purchases and embrace the benefits of the more fulfilling delayed gratification you'll get when building up your savings and repaying your debts.

Changing your spending and saving habits can be difficult at first, but the rewards are well worth the trouble. Try reducing the number and cost of everyday purchases by better allocating your money, clipping coupons for groceries or household products, or look for unique ways to make more money so you can comfortably cover all of your debts. Lifestyle changes that reduce your daily expenses will help you keep debt under control, too.

REDUCE DAILY EXPENSES

You might not be able to avoid paying for a repair for your car or medical bills, but debt doesn't always come from big purchases. A lot of debt builds up over time due to buying many smaller purchases without keeping track of your spending habits. You might put these small purchases on your credit card thinking nothing of it, then nearly faint when you see just how much you owe by the end of the month, or you might spend so much money on these smaller items that you don't have enough left in the bank account to pay off your debt. Either way, you'll need to make some changes to how much money you allow yourself to spend each day if you want to restore your credit and finally enjoy a debt-free life.

Think about your daily expenses and see where you can either cut back or go with a less expensive, generic version without much difference in quality. For example, smoking can be an expensive habit. If you can't manage to quit, you can instead go with cheaper brands, buy in bulk cartons, or roll your own to save some money. While quitting would save you the most money, making minor changes can result in major savings over time, especially if you're a heavy smoker who would otherwise be buying a pack or more each day. Tiny habit shifts have more significant ripple effects, so you don't have to live an entirely minimalist lifestyle to save a couple of hundred dollars each month. That said, avoid overspending even if you're buying cheaper products, as you might accidentally end up buying more than you need.

Here are some other ideas for reducing daily costs for a long-term increase in savings:

- Carpool to work with one of your coworkers to save on gas
- Use public transport if it's available in your area
- Improve your gas mileage by keeping your tires inflated and your car in good overall condition, but avoid unnecessary maintenance
- When possible, make coffee at home instead of going to a coffee shop
- When you are able, shop at the grocery store instead of the convenience store for lower prices and larger portions
- Limit yourself to one or two streaming subscription services at a time, or better yet, share and pool subscriptions together with friends/family so that each primary account holder purchases one streaming subscription and shares it amongst the group
- Review your paid memberships and other subscriptions regularly and decide whether you need to keep them
- Speak with your TV, internet, and cell providers and see where you can reduce costs

- Skip the gym membership and use free exercise videos on Youtube or go for a jog around the neighborhood
- Make a list before you go to the store and stick to it, so you only buy what you need
- Consider refurbished products instead of buying new
- Buy in bulk at warehouse club store likes Costco and Sam's Club when you can
- Turn off the lights when you leave your house
- Limit how often you get take-out to only a few times per month
- Buy generic food brands if there is no difference in nutritional value

Not every one of these methods will suit your lifestyle or individual needs, but you can save a ton just by choosing a handful of them and sticking to them for a month or two. Once you get into the habit of taking cost-cutting measures, you'll hopefully realize you didn't need that extra streaming service or the more expensive clothing brand after all. It will be easier than ever to keep your daily expenses down and save money.

Psychological Approaches to Cutting Spending

You might discover that when you try to adopt the above methods for cutting back on unnecessary spending, you have trouble sticking to them. In this case, you can use spending psychology to trick your mind into helping you save.

Remember that any advertisement's goal is to convince you that you need a particular product, whether you need it or not. Advertisers use psychological tricks of their own to convince you to buy. One such trick is only having the sale for a very short period or implying items will only be in stock for a limited time, encouraging you to buy quickly without taking the time to consider how much you need the product. When something looks pretty scarce and you're worried about it getting taken away, you're more likely to buy it. You can counteract this by being a little warier about what advertisers are trying to sell you. Force yourself to wait a little while before buying anything, even if it's just a few minutes and see if you still need it after you've had time to reconsider. There's something to be said about taking advantage of a good deal, but not if the seller is purposefully pressuring you into buying something you wouldn't otherwise have been interested in.

Another common approach is the envelope system. It involves designating cash for different types of purchases and setting the money aside in labeled envelopes. You would have envelopes for bills, the grocery store, entertainment, and of course, debt repayment. Once you've spent all the money in one, you're not allowed to spend anything else on that category of purchases until you refill all the envelopes at the end of the week or month. This is a good way to get into a light budgeting habit if you're not well-versed in it, allowing you to see how much money you've spent and how much you have left at any time. However, it might not be safe to have envelopes of cash lying around. You may not want to carry cash with you or simply prefer not to use paper money. In this case, consider creating a spreadsheet with different categories and set spending limits for each one, noting how much you spend with each purchase and how much you have left after.

Distinguishing Between Wants and Needs

We often tell ourselves we need certain things when it's really not the case. We might say something like, "I need to have the latest phone model or mine will be too slow," or "I absolutely need that new video game console." Usually, upon closer inspection and consideration, we discover that we don't really need these things as much as we'd originally thought.

Sure, you might need a cell phone to stay in touch with family or for work purposes, but you don't necessarily need the newest iPhone. You don't actually need a new video game console the month it comes out if you still play your older console. You desire these things, but they're not necessary for your ability to survive and take care of all your base needs. Of course, this doesn't mean you should never have anything that simply makes you happy, as self-fulfillment and stress relief are just as necessary as food and shelter. However, this does mean that if you decide you want something desperate enough and you're willing to spend a little extra for it, you need to figure out how to keep it within your budget or be willing to wait until you can actually afford it.

Let's look at TV as an example. Many people are "cutting the cord" and going cable-free these days to save money, but not everyone is willing to trade cable for streaming services just yet. You might still like having access to global and local news stations, sports channels, or even live TV in general, and you'd almost certainly have to give these up if you completely cut the cord. Still, this doesn't mean you have to keep spending as much on TV as you are now. You can still find ways to save, such as getting rid of channels you don't watch often enough to justify paying for them. You can also shop around for a different, cheaper cable provider in your area to lower your monthly bill to a more reasonable cost. You don't necessarily need to have cable, but if you want to keep it, you should be able to justify spending the money for it. If you simply can't afford it, it's better to downgrade or cut it out entirely until you've made some headway in paying off your debt. Once you have your finances under control, you can always re-subscribe to any services you cut out.

CLIP COUPONS

Another way to decrease your regular expenses is to look for sales and good deals before purchasing. Benjamin Franklin once said, "A penny saved is a penny earned," and that's undoubtedly true for couponing. You might think of coupon clipping as something only extreme couponers can do effectively, but just flipping through the mailer before you make your grocery list can save you a good chunk of change. Not only will you find discounts on products you wanted to buy anyway, but you might also swap out a product that's more expensive for one that's on sale, all because you took the time to look for coupons instead of just buying whatever first caught your eye at the grocery store.

That said, if you're going to clip coupons, you should be careful not to buy something you don't need or even really want just because it's on sale. Yes, a 50% off coupon for anything is an appealing offer, but 50% off is still more expensive than not buying it at all. If you're not going to use it, it's not worth buying, no matter how good the sale is.

Tips for Using Coupons Effectively

Cutting out a few coupons from your local grocery store's flyer is a good start, but many other methods will multiply your savings. For one, don't limit your couponing to what comes in the store flyers. Many businesses also put coupons in newspapers and magazines. Don't forget to check online, too, as many companies have digital-only coupons. You can find these in the official websites and apps for different businesses or from dedicated couponing platforms. Manufacturer websites may also offer coupons you can use at any store that offers their products. Check the price tags on the shelves when you're at the store, too, as there may be more deals, and you can more easily compare the values of different brands.

Digital coupons are especially convenient, as you don't have to physically clip the coupons and bring them to the store with you. All you need to do for most stores is make an account, load the coupons onto your account, and then give your account information at checkout. Some stores will also let you load the coupons onto your phone and scan it at the register, so you don't even have to go through an account creation process. This makes the coupons convenient for all involved—you're not fumbling with tiny strips of paper, there's no risk of leaving your coupons at home, and the computer will automatically apply all valid and applicable discounts. Most stores that use digital coupons offer their own apps, but there are also apps focused on compiling manufacturer coupons that could bring your savings down even further. You should be able to use both on different items in the same order without issue.

Apps and dedicated coupon websites are an excellent way to locate coupons too. They often have a much broader selection than the store's website, and they may feature coupons for stores that only send physical flyers or otherwise don't widely promote their deals. Like store apps, coupon apps offer a great way to keep couponing easy and portable, and for most websites, all you have to do is print out the coupons you want to use. Many of these sites also offer couponing tips and guidance from people who have been doing it for a while, so you can maximize your savings.

When you're clipping coupons, treat deals for perishable and non-perishable products differently. If a coupon offers savings on perishable food, consider if you'll eat it before it expires. There's no sense in buying two extra packages of something you already have just to save a dollar if you're going to end up throwing half away. Some perishable items can be frozen to extend their shelf-life, but always check the packaging to see if this is safe before doing so. On the other hand, there's little risk in using coupons for non-perishable items as long as they're something you use routinely, as you'll get to them eventually. You can buy an extra package of toilet paper even if you just bought one last week, since it's not going to spoil, and you might get a better deal now than if you waited the extra week. Buying non-perishable products ahead of schedule is excellent, but just be careful you're not hoarding. If you're looking to stockpile certain items, consider buying bulk coupon 'lots' from a coupon clipping service, which offers multiples of the same coupon, as long as the coupon doesn't state that it is one per customer.

Don't neglect a store's loyalty program either. Loyalty programs are a way for stores to thank you for shopping there frequently. They let you take advantage of additional deals in the store, and most of them are basically free to join, so there's no risk of wasting money. Once you sign up, pay attention to the labels on the aisles and look for products that offer an additional discount if you have the card. Then simply scan your card or use the phone number associated with your account to take advantage of these discounts. Most loyalty programs also let you earn points on your purchases, which can eventually be redeemed for money off your order once you've racked up enough of them. Getting a loyalty card for a store you frequent is a no-brainer.

Try not to be too picky about brands if possible. Different brands go on sale each week, so you'll be able to take advantage of more deals if you're okay using Hunt's ketchup instead of Heinz. Additionally, stores often offer better sales on their own brands, which you can sometimes combine with coupons for even more savings. In many cases, store-brand and name-brand products work just fine with little noticeable difference. For example, the active ingredient in Ibuprofen works the same whether you're buying a store-brand pain reliever or one of the big brands like Advil or Motrin and you'll usually get a larger quantity for the same or lower price if you go with the generic version.

Finally, keep your coupons somewhere convenient and well-organized. There's nothing worse than going to the store and realizing you left all your coupons at home. Keep them somewhere you'll have access to them, such as in your car or inside your purse or wallet if you don't have too many. Organize your coupons in a way that helps you find what you're looking for as efficiently as possible. Some people prefer to order by the type of product, while others sort by where the aisles are in the store or when the coupons are set to expire. Flip through your stack of coupons regularly and check for any that have expired, so you don't confuse them for valid ones. This also helps you avoid overstuffing your coupon binder, wallet, or wherever you choose to store them.

STRETCH YOUR INCOME

If you can't adjust your expenses any further, try focusing your efforts on adjusting your income. Sometimes you may not be making enough money to cover all of your bills and still have some cash left over to put in the bank. If you don't make a change, you're going to stay stuck in debt limbo, never able to dig yourself out of the hole completely. However, depending on your situation, you might not be able to get a raise or a higher-paying job right now. Even so, you can still increase your income through other means and use it as effectively as possible.

Start a Side Hustle

If you're looking for a way to make a little extra cash, you might consider turning a part-time hobby into another source of revenue. Do you enjoy drawing and painting? Consider selling your art online or taking commission work. Are you crafty? Open an Etsy store and fill it with handmade gifts. Do you love to cook or bake? Start your own catering business in your neighborhood. Your side hustle doesn't necessarily have to be a hobby, but it should be something you're interested in and that you enjoy doing, as you'll have to add it onto your regular daily routine. Don't choose something so exhausting you can't keep up with your full-time job.

Other common examples of side hustles include tutoring, photography, video editing, gardening for neighbors, housekeeping services, and pet sitting. Jobs you can do digitally are ideal, as 'gig' sites like Fiverr and TaskRabbit let you market to people interested in your services from all around the world.

Sell What You Don't Need

When you get into the habit of buying less, you'll quickly notice that you likely have many things lying around the house that you don't use anymore. Whether these are jackets you grew out of a few years ago and haven't worn since, knick-knacks that are only collecting dust on the shelf or that guitar you never really learned how to play, it's time to get rid of all the junk and clutter. You don't have to go full minimalist, but as a general rule, if you haven't touched it in over a year, it's probably not something you need to keep.

As the saying goes, one man's trash is another man's treasure. Tossing all of these items in the garbage would be wasteful, especially if they're still in good condition. Put them up for sale, either by holding a garage sale outside your house or list them in an online marketplace. Facebook has its own marketplace that connects you to people who live nearby, apps like Letgo and Nextdoor let you find buyers without much effort, and sites like thredUP and Mercari are great for getting rid of old clothes.

Just make sure what you're selling is in decent condition or describe any damages in your advertisement before someone shows up to buy it.

Don't forget to do your due diligence and find out if anything you own is more valuable than you think. You might find the old sewing machine you got from your grandmother is considered an antique and worth far more than the $20 you were going to charge. You'll want to know this before you make the sale rather than after. Price shop at online marketplaces or in second-hand retail stores so you can choose a fair price for anything you resell.

Double Check Your Tax Withholding

When you first start a job, you fill out tax forms so the government knows how much money they should take out of each paycheck as an estimate for your yearly taxes. How much you owe in taxes can change for a number of reasons, including getting married or divorced, having a child or another dependent, retiring, buying a home, filing for bankruptcy, making more or less money, taking various deductions, or when tax laws change. Don't forget that you can claim yourself as a dependent on your withholding form, which means you'll have less of your paycheck withheld. However, it doesn't change how much you're actually paying in taxes, just when you have access to this money. If the government withholds too little from your paychecks, you'll owe a hefty bill come tax season. If they withhold too much, you'll be missing out on money that should be in your pocket until you get your tax refund.

To change your withholding, you'll have to fill out a W-4 form with your updated information. Then submit this form to your employer so they can apply it to your paychecks.

9

THE CREDIT CARD EDGE

"Spend extravagantly on the things you love and cut costs mercilessly on the things you don't."

— RAMIT SETHI

When you have a history of misusing credit cards and ending up in debt, it's easy to see the cards as the problem and try to swear them off entirely. You might convince yourself that credit cards will only ever be bad news and there's no way to use them to your benefit. It's equally likely that you finally start decreasing your debt, but immediately go back to putting way too many purchases on your credit cards, thereby failing to prevent yourself from making the same mistakes all over again. Neither of these methods will help you build a healthy relationship with credit.

If you want to start making more intelligent use of your credit cards, you need to begin by seeing them as tools that are neither good nor bad. You can use them to help your financial situation or hurt it. They can just as easily assist you in buying more expensive, necessary items as they can help you pile up mountains of debt. The only difference between these two endpoints is how you use your credit cards. Responsible credit card use is key if you're trying to reset your finances and rebuild your credit from the ground up.

This includes maximizing the benefits you get from your cards, such as cashback, deals, and points. It also includes avoiding predatory lending practices that are designed to saddle you with unreasonable amounts of debt. Instead, look for cards that will help you pursue and achieve your financial goals.

AVOID PAYDAY LOANS AND CASH ADVANCES

When you're in a bind, payday loans and cash advances may seem like the only way out. You can't pay off your current debt and other bills or you're in a financial emergency with no savings, so you turn to these two options as a quick fix that you insist you can pay off later. However, the problems they cause are never worth the limited amount of good they do in the short term. Most people who take out these kinds of loans end up in more debt than they started with, making it incredibly easy to get themselves into a situation they can't afford to get out of.

While payday loans and cash advances often have similar outcomes, they're used for different purposes. A payday loan, theoretically, gets you access to your next paycheck sooner than usual. When you take out the loan, you write a postdated check for your next payday in the amount of most or all of your salary, and in exchange, you receive a certain portion of your paycheck as the loan balance. For example, let's say you have an important bill due on Tuesday, but you don't get paid until next Friday. You write a $1,000 check to be cashed the following Monday to give your paycheck time to clear when you can use your paycheck to repay the loan. In exchange, you get $700 upfront to pay off that bill, with the payday loan company keeping the remaining $300 as their service fee. You generally won't get your whole paycheck and you may have to pay some interest on the loan, but this is rarely where the expenses stop, as you'll soon learn.

Credit card cash advances rely on similarly dubious practices. Cash advances let you borrow money against your credit card so you can get a short-term cash loan at an ATM or bank. You can take out a portion of your remaining credit line as cash, usually no more than a few hundred dollars. While this is convenient, it can get incredibly costly, too.

The Problem with These Loans

Maybe payday loans and cash advances don't offer the best rates, but are they really so bad? These kinds of loans can be far more damaging than they appear to be on the surface. For starters, they're typically only used by people already struggling with debt and other financial problems. The terms of these loans aren't ideal and you probably wouldn't agree to them if you had any other option. But payday loans and cash advances don't check your credit for eligibility, which means you'll have a much easier time getting them, even if borrowing money isn't a good idea with your current DTI ratio.

Additionally, payday loans have you essentially give up your paycheck in exchange for a fraction of its value while also requiring you to write out a check ahead of time, which can leave you trapped in a cycle of taking out additional payday loans and diminishing your income. If you can't pay it back because you had to spend the money elsewhere or you can't pay the additional incredibly high interest on the money you received, you'll end up accruing more interest and debt as you keep rolling the loan forward every few weeks. Let's say you take out a payday loan to cover a financial emergency. Your original loan is for $500 with an additional $50 interest. In two weeks, all the money goes toward the emergency expense and the remainder is used up by your regular expenses, leaving you without money to pay back the $550. This continues for months, as you can never quite catch up to the rapidly increasing interest, and every two weeks, you add another $50 charge to your balance. The debt will become insurmountable before long and most payday loan companies aren't shy about taking you to court over what you owe.

Cash advances are often just as bad since they also have short loan terms and very high interest rates that make payday loans so dangerous. There's typically no grace period, so interest starts to build up right away. Additionally, cash advances have many associated fees that can balloon the price even further. Your card issuer might charge you a percentage or flat fee, and the ATM you use will also charge their own processing fee, further increasing how much you owe and making it harder to pay back.

In either situation, you're left with a mountain of debt and no real savings to pay it off. This is far from a responsible borrowing practice if you want to use credit effectively. These kinds of loans are essentially designed to force you into a tough spot when you're already having trouble managing your money and they're a sorry replacement for real credit with fair terms. Avoid these two options at all cost.

TAKE ADVANTAGE OF POINTS AND CASH BACK

If you want to have a healthier relationship with credit, you need to reconsider how you use it. Yes, credit cards can be costly when they're misused, but this isn't the only way to use them. Many people who spend responsibly get to take advantage of the great benefits credit cards offer, such as points and cashback. Making the best possible use of these will help you save money on every purchase and reduce your overall amount of debt, making it easier to pay back at the end of the billing period.

Points and cashback are two excellent ways to save on everyday purchases. Points can be redeemed for discounts on various products and services, depending on your card. Many credit cards offer airline miles as a reward, which can save you anywhere from hundreds to thousands of dollars if you fly often. Other cards may offer points that can be applied to hotels, certain merchandise, and gift cards. You can also get cashback rewards on many different cards for common purchases like gas, restaurants, groceries, and purchases made at certain stores. Some cards offer set cashback rates of around 1-3% of the purchase price for different categories. In contrast, others may provide higher cashback amounts in exchange for a selection of purchases that rotate every few months. Certain cards offer 1% cashback on all purchases in addition to those that are eligible for higher cashback rewards.

If you play your cards right, you can reduce how much you owe on every statement. Let's say you want to buy a new TV and put it on your credit card, and one of your card issuers is currently offering 5% cashback on all purchases made at Best

Buy next month. You could buy a $600 TV right away from any store, put it on a card without any cashback, and be on the hook for the full $600 at the end of the billing period as well as any accrued interest without a grace period. Or you can put up with your old TV for another month, buy the same TV at Best Buy, and get $30 in cashback. Most lenders will let you apply the cashback you've earned directly to your bill, so you'll only have to pay $570 for the TV if you still have a grace period. It's not an incredible difference, but if you ignore it, you're leaving money on the table, and even small amounts can add up over time. The same is true for using points on applicable purchases. Always review the reward policies of any new card before you sign up for it and do some shopping around to find the one that offers you the greatest advantages.

How to Earn Points

Cashback is a fairly straightforward method for returning money to your pocket, but you might not be as well-versed in how points work. You can earn points through different forms depending on your card. Some lenders let you earn extra points through referrals, such as spending a certain amount of money within a few months of getting the card, reaching milestones, or adding an authorized user to your account. Still, customarily, points will come from routine purchases. Typically, one dollar spent translates to one point. Some cards offer better point conversion rates on different spending categories such as gas or food, while others offer points for purchases exclusive to these set categories.

You can check what kind of benefits your points qualify you for on the lender's website. Once you've racked up enough points, you can convert them into different rewards offered by your cardholder. While you want to earn rewards as you go, this doesn't mean you should spend a lot more to reach them faster, as the debt you later find yourself in might outpace your savings. Instead, either continue spending as usual or make minor adjustments to your spending habits if this won't break the bank. As always, refrain from spending outside of your means, no matter the savings.

Points Versus Cashback

If you're trying to decide between a card that offers points and one that offers cashback, base your decision on which option you would use more often with your current lifestyle. Neither is inherently better than the other, but it's probably not a smart move to go for a card offering airline miles when you rarely travel. On the other hand, if you have a job that requires you to fly frequently, a card that prioritizes airline miles could save you far more money than one that just offers a small percentage of some of your purchases as cashback. Another important factor to consider is flexibility. Points typically only apply to a handful of things, while cashback can be applied to any purchase. The money you get back might be less than what you would save using points, but you have the freedom to use it wherever you like, as opposed to being stuck redeeming it at hotels or airlines. While both cashback and point cards frequently offer sign-on bonuses, point cards' bonuses tend to be larger. You may also get additional discounts when you redeem your points at certain businesses.

The card that works best for you will be different from what works best for someone else. There is no clear, correct answer to this question. Evaluate the pros and cons of each type of card as it applies to your situation and determine which one will help you use your credit cards as responsibly as possible. The more you start taking advantage of cashback and points, the better you'll be at staying out of debt and turning credit into a helpful tool rather than a dangerous temptation.

Maximize Point and Cashback Benefits with Good Habits

Good borrowing habits will ensure you make the most of your points or cashback. Getting money back for your purchases is great, but it should never encourage you to make unnecessary purchases. Yes, you might save some money, but if you're buying things you don't need, you're wasting far more money than you're saving. Many cards have a lower intro APR, with some as low as 0% for a few months, but when this wears off, you'll have to pay back any interest you would have accrued during that time if your balance isn't already at zero. If you can afford to pay them off at the end of the billing period, then feel free to make big purchases that give you lots of rewards. But if you end up saving less from points or cashback than you pay in interest, you're losing money. It's better to wait and save up for these purchases instead, ideally waiting until you can afford to pay them off entirely at the end of the billing period.

Remember to take advantage of the grace period, too, if available. If you time your purchases right, you can give yourself nearly two months before the bill is due, which should provide you with ample time to pay these purchases off in full with the assistance of cashback.

Always consider your spending habits before getting any card that comes with an annual fee. Some of these cards offer the best points or cashback rewards, but it's not always worth it if you can't take full advantage of those bonuses. First, can you afford to pay the fee each year without issue? Make sure to budget extra for the month the fee is charged, so you aren't caught off guard. Next, do you think you'll spend enough that the cashback you get will outweigh the fee? There's no sense in signing up for a card with an annual fee if you won't be able to earn enough throughout the year to make that fee worth it. Ensure you're not overspending to hit this mark either, so you won't end up in debt once again. You should stay within your budget and still comfortably make enough in cashback and other rewards to pay for the card. If not, it's not worth getting that card and you should prioritize credit cards that offer decent benefits without annual fees instead.

10

BUDGET ALLOWANCES FOR A DEBT-FREE LIFE

"It is much easier to put existing resources to better use, than to develop resources where they do not exist."

— GEORGE SOROS

Whether you're still working your way out of debt or you're debt-free and want to stay that way, a budget will help you keep track of your finances while keeping an eye on where your money is going. When you don't budget, you drastically increase your risk of overspending. It's easy to not notice just how much you've spent if you make many small purchases. They don't seem like much at the time, but later, you might get your credit card bill and find out you've spent hundreds of dollars on entertainment costs alone. If your income doesn't support this lifestyle, it can quickly balloon into a big problem as the out of control spending and interest sends you deeper into debt.

Maybe you've tried to budget before, but found that it's hard to stick to because you just can't seem to hold yourself accountable or because the budget was too general and it didn't really help you save money. You might have prioritized the wrong spending categories, causing you to spend way too much on unnecessary purchases and far too little on important costs like bills, paying off debt, and contributing to your savings. Budgets can fail for a number of different reasons, but that doesn't mean budgeting itself is wrong or that it isn't something you're capable of doing. It just means you haven't found the right style budget for you yet. You can create and stick to a budget that suits your income, lifestyle, and individual preferences. Budgeting sets you up for success, so you want to build a strong foundation before you start stacking things on top of it.

WHAT IS A PERSONAL BUDGET?

Before you can start making your budget, you should know exactly what it is. A budget is a tool you use to estimate your monthly expenses and divide your income so you can comfortably pay for everything. It's a way to curb excessive spending without putting all of your money under lock and key.

In short, it's not a set of restraints, but a roadmap that gives you directions for achieving financial freedom.

Your budget is an action plan that's meant to help you minimize your expenses and maximize your savings. When you budget right, you'll significantly improve your financial health and keep your spending in check. You can budget for any length of time, but most people find it helpful to keep things small and work with a biweekly or monthly budget when making a personal financial plan. You can also budget for any income level, whether you have a fairly high-paying job and you tend to spend too much money on the wrong things, or you have a low-paying job, and you're trying to make ends meet as best as you can. Budgeting is especially helpful for those months where your income is lower than you expected, such as if you worked fewer hours than usual or if you had a financial emergency come up that monopolized your funds. When you lay all of your income sources and your expenses out in front of you, you'll be able to make smarter, more informed decisions about which expenses you should prioritize and how you want to divide up your money.

When you create and follow a personal budget, you give yourself more significant control over your finances. The more you know about how much you're making and where that money is going, the easier it will be for you to reroute that money to where it is most needed. When creating a budget, you'll write down different expense categories like food, clothes, entertainment, rent/mortgage, utilities, other bills, debt payments, and savings. Then you'll decide how you want to split your income between these different expenses, starting with the most important ones before allocating the rest. There are many different budgeting methods, so not every budget will look the same. To set the appropriate spending goals, test various techniques to find the best fit for you.

Budgeting Misconceptions

There are many misconceptions about budgets that could make you more hesitant to use them. For example, many people believe living on a budget means you have to restrict your spending altogether and you can't make any purchases that are nonessential and/or for personal enjoyment. This is a false concept because in truth, budgeting can help you spend on dispensable purchases in a way that doesn't break the bank. There's no need to cut out the occasional fun night with friends or going to a restaurant for date night. You only need to look at these expenses within the context of the rest of your budget and use this information to prevent yourself from going overboard. These kinds of costs are perfectly fine in moderation. It's only when they start eating away at the money you should be putting toward your bills that they become a problem. You don't have to give them up entirely, though you may have to cut back on them a little if you want to become debt-free. For example, if cutting out the things you love means misery, then budget for a small amount. Buy a gift card for $25 and when it's drained, you're done visiting your favorite barista or store for that month.

Another common myth is that budgets take too long to make. While you may have to spend a little while on them when you're first starting out, before long, you'll get into the rhythm, and future budgets will hardly take any time at all. Set aside about an hour the first time you make a budget to review your spending history thoroughly. The good news is that you only have to make one budget for the length of time the budget covers, whether that's weekly, biweekly, or monthly. Even an hour a week shouldn't eat into your free time too much and given how much you stand to benefit from budgeting, it's well worth that hour. Time may be money, but spending a little bit of time budgeting will save you a lot of money.

Many people assume that tracking their spending is a suitable replacement for budgeting. While it's certainly better than doing nothing at all, it's ultimately far less effective than budgeting. For one, tracking your spending is reactive, not proactive. You're recording what you do, but you're not adjusting your spending habits based on this information. Once you've spent $200 more than you intended in dining out expenses for the month and whether you write it down or not, you can't get that money back. Budgeting helps you prevent making unnecessary purchases before you make them, which gives you a better opportunity to change your spending habits. Additionally, if you're already tracking your spending, budgeting should be your natural next move. It's effortless to transition this into a budget, as you already know how you're spending your money and you just need to make adjustments to ensure all your bases are covered.

WHY BUDGETING IS IMPORTANT

A budget is the single best way to improve a tumultuous financial situation. While every other method we've discussed so far has been mainly focused on paying off your debts so you can be debt-free, a budget is your one-way ticket to not just getting debt-free but also staying debt-free. Time and again, people claw their way out of debt by cutting back on other expenses, obtaining loans, or declaring bankruptcy. But they don't change any of their spending habits and in a few months, they're back in debt, and they have to repeat the same process all over again. If you've experienced this, you're not alone. Perhaps the reason why you ended up sliding back into debt, barring any substantial unforeseen emergencies, is that you weren't aware of how to utilize good spending habits that would have given you a leg up and kept you from overborrowing time and time again. When you follow a budget, you're giving yourself the tools you need to succeed and live a life completely free from the stresses of debt.

Sure, a budget isn't going to multiply your income. It's not going to make your car insurance payments cheaper or knock down the mortgage on your house, but there's very little that will allow you to do those things, as they're largely out of your control in most circumstances. They become even less attainable when you're already struggling with money and credit problems. Focus on the things you can control, such as where and how you decide to spend your money. Budgeting is your secret weapon because it redirects your focus to your expenses, which is where it is needed most. It sets you up with good spending and borrowing habits that you can continue to use whether you're making $10,000 a year or $100,000. This makes it invaluable if you really want to stay out of debt permanently.

How Budgeting Changes the Way You Think About Money

If you had to guess where your money goes every month, how accurate do you think that assessment would be without looking up your expenses? When we think about our spending habits, we tend to give a lot of weight to large lump-sum expenses. For example, if your mortgage is $1,200 each month, you might automatically assume that's where all your money is going. But let's say you make about $40,000 a year, which is about $3,300 a month. This means $2,100, nearly two-thirds of your paycheck, is going to other expenses. If you find yourself coming up short and you can't afford to pay your credit card bill, even if it's much cheaper than your monthly mortgage, you might wonder where the rest of that money is going.

How can your biggest expense take up so little of your income and yet you're still in debt? Even though it may be the largest single expense, it may not be the greatest strain on your finances. You have to pay for dozens of other purchases, both big and small. If you spend $200 on groceries every week for four weeks, you've already spent $800. Spend $20 every day on miscellaneous purchases like coffee and Uber rides to and from work and that's another $600. You're already paying $1,400 from these two categories of expenses alone, outpacing how much you spend on housing without factoring in the countless other bills and various expenses that might eat into your paycheck. Without a budget, you may not be aware of the damage these small purchases are doing to your wallet as they add up over time.

Budgeting is the solution to this problem. When you write out how much everything costs and how you plan to spend your money, you'll notice expenses getting out of control. Your budget will highlight instances of overspending so you can change your habits and look for more cost-effective solutions. For example, if you're spending too much on Uber rides to work, you might try to carpool with a coworker or get an earlier start and walk if you live close enough. If you can't reduce your spending here, you can look for other areas to cut back instead. You won't know that these costs are becoming a problem unless you budget for them and without knowing, you likely won't change your spending habits.

Budgeting also encourages you to give each dollar its own purpose. When you create a budget, you allocate all your income to specific types of purchases or savings. No dollar goes unaccounted for, which means every dollar is equally important. Overspending in one category means you won't have enough for another. This also means you can dedicate money specifically for entertainment, so you can spend your disposable income without guilt since you've already accounted for it in your budget. You'll know where all your money is going, so you know how much you can afford to spend on any one thing.

Budgeting for Unexpectedly Low Income

While everyone can benefit from budgeting no matter how much money they make, it's imperative if you find yourself in a tight spot with less income than you're used to. This means you probably have to make some changes to your spending habits. Purchases you could comfortably afford before might become extreme burdens on your bank account now. Even though you're spending as much as you were before that pay cut or unexpected expense, you're now living above your means. Reviewing your budget will help you make the changes you need to live with limited income, whether this is a temporary problem or a more long-term one. Even a month or two without your regular income can put you in a lot of debt if you start relying too heavily on credit. Budgeting will help you avoid this unfortunate outcome as best you can with good planning.

If you need to cut back, start by calculating the absolute minimum amount of money you can live on. Then decide which expenses are the most important and which ones you could give up for a short while. For example, paying your mortgage or rent should be a top priority, as you could lose your home if you don't. Going to the movie theater is far less important in comparison. Even if it is fun, there are many other ways you can find entertaining, local activities that are entirely free and many inexpensive or free, ways you can watch other movies instead. It's not a necessity, so you should cut back on these incidental expenses first when money is tight.

If you've written out a budget with only the necessities and you still can't afford to pay for it all, you may need to look into other sources of income to make up the difference, such as doing part-time work or asking for an advance in pay if your company offers it. Since you have a budget, you know how much money you can live on and still get by while you search for a more permanent solution. Financial troubles can be incredibly stressful and damaging to your well-being in a number of different ways and you don't want to make this any worse than it has to be. With a budget, you can use your money as effectively as possible, thereby limiting your reliance on credit to see you through difficult times.

MANAGING YOUR BUDGET

Now that you know why budgeting is vital and how it can help you take control of your finances, let's look at how to actually create a budget that accounts for your financial situation. Your budget should first and foremost be unique to you and your needs. If you have a large family, you'll probably have to spend a higher portion of your income on groceries than someone who lives alone. Suppose you're dealing with credit card debt or you're trying to pay off some newly consolidated loans before they accrue a lot of interest. In that case, you'll likely have to dedicate a larger portion of your money to pay down debt than you would otherwise. Consider your own unique concerns as you begin budgeting, as everyone's situation is different.

One notable difference between everyone's budgets is how much of a priority saving is for you. Some people prefer first to allocate money to all other categories and then put the remainder in their savings account, while others make savings a set percentage of their income and make sure they put money in before they dip into their disposable income. In general, having some savings is important because it serves as a buffer for any financial emergencies you may encounter. A sudden charge of $400 can either be devastating or no issue at all, and this is entirely dependent on how much money you have saved. That said, if you're already contributing to your retirement fund from your paycheck and have about three to six months' worth of living expenses in your emergency fund, you should be okay to make additional savings a lower priority. If you don't yet have an emergency fund, you'll probably want to prioritize it over less necessary purchases.

One possible way to do so is the 50/30/20 rule, which provides general guidelines for dividing your income. According to this rule, it's recommended that you "reserve 50% of your budget for essentials like rent and food, 30% for discretionary spending, and at least 20% for savings" (Weliver, 2021, para. 4). Of course, if you're creating a budget, it's a good idea to go into more detail, but these numbers can point you in the right direction. Putting away about 20% of your income for a rainy day means that no matter what big shakeups you run into in the future, you'll have the savings to handle them. Again, there are many cases where you might not be able to follow this rule. If you are trying to pay down debt, it may be more cost effective to focus on that before contributing this much to your savings. You might instead choose to save just 5% or to save $50 every month or another amount that's manageable for you. On the other hand, if your income far outweighs your expenses, you can probably save an even more significant allocation. Use the 50/30/20 'rule' as a guideline and adjust it to fit your current situation.

Set Goals

Financial goals can vary from person to person. Maybe your primary goal is paying off your high-interest debts first. This means you should devote a larger chunk of your budget to debt payments until you've regained control over your credit and improved your credit score. Maybe you're debt-free and you want to stay that way, so you want to limit your credit card use and cut back on unnecessary spending. You should instead prioritize savings and start spending less on entertainment and clothes. Your goals serve as your purpose for budgeting and your motivation to stick to your budget. A goal like "becoming debt-free" is a more powerful motivator than simply going through the motions without any thought as to why better spending habits matter to you. As time progresses, you'll develop a better picture of what you want to achieve and why; only then will you be more committed to following your budget and achieving these goals.

Calculate Income and Expenses

Before you can start allocating funds, you need to know how much you have available if your only source of income is your job, so you need to write down your monthly net income. If your income fluctuates each month, either because you're paid hourly or have alternate sources of income like investments or odd jobs, work with a number on the lower end of your earnings. Your budget will be much more critical during the months where your income is lower.

It's helpful if you also had a reasonable estimate of how much you typically spend on additional purchases to create an exceptionally functional budget. If you spend $150 on groceries every week, budgeting just $200 for groceries for the entire month isn't going to work. You can cut back, but you need to be realistic about your expectations. If you're already tracking your spending, then you can use your spending history to calculate your current average expenses. If not, spend about a month writing down whenever you make a purchase, keeping track of how much things cost, and recording them according to the expense type. Once the month is up, see how much you spent on different categories like gas, groceries, bills, entertainment, and more. This will give you your starting figures for your expenses, which you can then compare to your income to see whether you're on the right track or need to make some changes.

Review Your Spending and Expense Habits

In an average month without budgeting, how good are you at living within your means? Ideally, your expenses should be far below your income, with plenty of your money going to savings. However, if you're paying off a lot of debt or if you're used to making purchases without spending conservatively, this probably isn't the case.

A review of your spending gives you an idea of how you'll need to adjust those habits as you create your budget. Look for areas where you spend far more than you need to. You probably can't bring your mortgage payments down without talking to your bank, but you have a lot more control over how much you spend on items that aren't necessities. If you're way over budget, identify the most extensive problem areas so you can fix them.

Analyze and Adjust Habits

Once you know where your spending weaknesses are, you can adopt habits to address them. It's great to modify your budget, so you're not encouraging excessive spending, but you need to actually put this into practice for it to have any real effect. Excessive spending is a habit that builds up over time and you'll need to replace it with habits that promote more thoughtful spending.

Remember to reduce daily expenses with good habits like clipping coupons and thinking about purchases before you make them. Try to integrate these habits into your day-to-day life, and always be on the lookout for harmful habits like eating at restaurants too often or using "retail therapy." Think about whether a routine helps you achieve a financial goal or inhibits you from achieving it, then take action to correct any habits that get in your way.

Fully Commit to the Plan

At the end of the day, a budget only works if you follow it. You can set yourself up for success, but if you don't actually reduce your spending and redistribute your income as you planned in your budget, nothing about your financial situation will change. That said, committing can sometimes be tricky because you might not see positive results right away. A single month of following a budget isn't going to immediately fix all of your problems, but it's the start of a good habit, and like all habits, it has a cumulative effect. If you stick to the plan you've laid out for yourself and stay within your budget parameters, the little changes will add up over time.

You'll also need to commit to taking your finances more seriously as a whole if you want to achieve absolute financial freedom. Careless spending and a lack of preparation got you into a mess with debt originally. If you don't adopt better spending and borrowing habits, you'll only end up in the same place again a year or two down the line. When you start making positive changes to how you utilize credit, how much you save, and how you approach debt issues, you'll keep yourself out of financial trouble in the future so you can pursue and maintain a debt-free life.

CONCLUSION

Getting out of debt, no matter how much you owe, all starts with making a payment. On its own, a single payment may not drastically reduce the amount of money you owe. However, if you turn this payment into a habit and adopt other positive spending and saving behaviors, you'll be well on your way to becoming debt-free. Remember that it all comes down to taking action.

Throughout this book, you've been introduced to various strategies for reassessing and tackling your debt. You've discovered how strategies like peer-to-peer lending, negotiating with creditors, and debt consolidation can help you get better rates on your loans, thereby allowing you to pay them off in a reasonable amount of time. You learned how to locate errors on credit reports and dispute them to improve your credit health, as well as how to raise your credit score, so you qualify for better card and loan terms. You've seen examples of how you can adopt healthier habits for managing your finances, including using credit cards responsibly, budgeting, and making the most of grace periods. You've also learned about the power of making payments and chipping away at your debt to bring your balance down over time.

When it comes to debt, there are very few, if any, reliable shortcuts. Everything you borrow has to be paid back one way or another, and if not, it will seriously harm your credit and future lending opportunities. The longer you wait to do something about your debt, the worse it will get. Don't wait any longer. Start implementing some of the strategies discussed in this book as soon as possible, even if all you're capable of right now is making a single payment. Take action on your debts today to pave the way to financial freedom in your future.

If you found the advice for becoming debt-free within this book helpful, please consider leaving an honest review on Amazon. This lets other people who are also struggling with debt know that this is a reliable resource, and like you, they'll be able to start their journey toward debt relief.

HOW TO GET THE MOST OUT OF
THIS BOOK

If you're genuinely curious, willing to make changes, and take action, you can be on your way towards a debt-free future. To help you on your journey, I have created a free workbook that includes an easy to use budgeting sheet & debt calculator to determine your debt-free date. Use this tool to guide you in accomplishing your goals.

To get the most out of this book, sign up now by visiting the link below:

https://allenanything.com

REFERENCES

Bayers, C. (1999, Mar. 1). *The inner Jeff Bezos.* Wired. https://www.wired.com/1999/03/bezos-3/

Chen, J. (2020, Oct. 25). *Debt.* Investopedia. https://www.investopedia.com/terms/d/debt.asp

Comoreanu, A. (2012, Oct. 3). *More issuers found guilty of deceptive credit card practices, find out how to avoid becoming a victim.* WalletHub. https://wallethub.com/edu/cc/credit-card-deceptive-practices/25698

Federal Trade Commission (2012, Aug.). *Lost or Stolen Credit, ATM, and Debit Cards.* https://www.consumer.ftc.gov/articles/pdf-0075-lost-or-stolen-credit-atm-and-debit-cards.pdf

Foreman, G. (2012, Aug. 16). *What it means when a debt is 'written off.'* Creditcards.com https://www.creditcards.com/credit-card-news/written-off-statute-limitations-debt-1580/

Hipp, D. (2020, Nov. 13). *How to dispute an error on your credit report.* Credit Karma. https://www.creditkarma.com/credit-cards/i/dispute-error-credit-report

Holzhauer, B. (2020, Nov. 10). *How to dispute a charge: Everything you should know.* ValuePenguin. https://www.valuepenguin.com/disputing-credit-card-purchases

Kagan, J. (2021, Jan. 28). *Debt collector.* Investopedia. https://www.investopedia.com/terms/d/debt-collector.asp

Kennedy, J. F. (1961, Jan. 20). Presidential inaugural address [Speech audio recording]. American Rhetoric. https://www.americanrhetoric.com/speeches/jfkinaugural.htm

Kissell, C. & Hicks, C. (2020, Dec. 9). *APR vs. interest rate: What's the difference?* U.S. News. https://loans.usnews.com/articles/apr-vs-interest-rate-whats-the-difference

Kiyosaki, R. (2015). *Rich dad poor dad: What the rich teach their kids about money that the poor and middle class do not!* Plata Publishing.

O'Shea, B. (2020, Dec. 16). *Minimize credit score damage from late payments.* Nerdwallet. https://www.nerdwallet.com/article/finance/late-bill-payment-reported

Ramsey, D. (2002). *Financial peace revisited: New chapters on marriage, singles, kids, and families.* Penguin Books.

Ramsey, D. (2021, Feb. 23). *The truth about debt consolidation.* Dave Ramsey. https://www.daveramsey.com/blog/debt-consolidation-truth

Rathner, S. & McGuire, V. C. (2020, May 29). *Credit card grace period puts interest on hold.* Nerdwallet. https://www.nerdwallet.com/article/credit-cards/credit-card-grace-period

Robbins, T. [@TonyRobbins]. (2016, Mar. 1). *The real joy in life comes from finding your true purpose and aligning it with what you do every single day* [Tweet]. Twitter. https://twitter.com/TonyRobbins/status/704759561987620864

Rockefeller, J. D. Jr. (2015). *John D. Rockefeller on making money: Advice and words of wisdom on building and sharing wealth.* Skyhorse Publishing, Inc.

Sethi, R. (2019). *I will teach you to be rich, second edition: No guilt. No excuses. No BS. Just a 6-week program that works.* Workman Publishing.

Soros, G. (2007). *Age of fallibility: Consequences of the war on terror.* PublicAffairs.

Weliver, D. (2021, Mar. 19). *How much should you save every month?* Money Under 30. https://www.moneyunder30.com/percentage-of-income-should-you-save-every-month

www.ingramcontent.com/pod-product-compliance
Lightning Source LLC
Chambersburg PA
CBHW021458180326
41458CB00051B/6876/J